Living with God in Loss

LIVING WITH
GOD IN LOSS

ERNEST DYSON

Ernest Dyson
Dec, 1992

BROADMAN PRESS
Nashville, Tennessee

Unless otherwise noted Scripture quotations are from the
Revised Standard Version of the Bible, copyrighted 1946,
1952, © 1971, 1973. Scripture quotations marked (NEB)
are from *The New English Bible*. Copyright © The Dele-
gates of the Oxford University Press and the Syndics of the
Cambridge University Press, 1961, 1970. Reprinted by permission. Scripture quotations marked (NIV) are from the
HOLY BIBLE New Internation Version, copyright ©
1978, New York Bible Society. Used by permission.

Library of Congress Cataloging-in-Publication Data

Dyson, Ernest, 1926-
  Living with God in loss.

  1. Consolation.   I. Title.
BV4905.2.D97   1989   248.8'6   88-24125
ISBN 0-8054-5443-8 (pbk.)

Dedicated

To the glory of God—
whose love brought forth life;
To Ernest Allen Dyson (1950-1986)—
whose love brought forth this book;
To my family, all of you—
in whose love I live.

"Here are my mother and my brothers.
For whoever does the will of my Father
in heaven is my brother and sister and
mother" (Matt. 12:50, NIV).

CONTENTS

Introduction

In the course of living, we all lose things. Some of what is lost is of little consequence, and we pay the privation no mind. At other times life bruises us deeply by taking that in which we have some deep personal investment, something that strikes at our sense of security and identity. Such profound loss can occur in financial disasters, when we are dismissed from a job for reasons over which we have no control, when intimate friends move away so that the close association we enjoyed is no longer possible, or when we suffer a marital separation through divorce. Even illness or the aging process can diminish our physical and mental powers so that we experience a loss of ability to do what we used to do and to be what we previously were. The loss of a loved one through physical death is probably the ultimate example of such privation.

When we are hurt by events over which we have no control, events in which we feel we are innocent victims, we may become angry and confused. If we are people of faith, who are we to be angry with but God who is in charge of it all? Yet, we believe that God is loving and would not be unjust, so we are confused. In such a dilemma, we thrash about for understanding, and people arrive at various explanations to make sense of loss.

Some truly faithful folk exonerate God by attributing the traumatic event to their own upbuilding. "God sends us adversity to strengthen us," they claim. Others take the view that "this is a terrible punishment that I must suffer for my sinfulness." Still others hold God guilty and do not want to let the Creator off without blame; these lash out in their hurt and turn completely away from that which they thought they believed. Many simply remain docile, but confused, not wanting to believe God intends hurt. Nevertheless, they are not fully convinced that the Almighty hasn't done just that. These people ask the endless *why's* to which they receive no convincing answers.

All of us feel anger when we are hurt, especially when we feel unjustly victimized. We may cover that anger with ideas that God wounds us to make us strong or to punish us. We may express that anger by denouncing and turning away from God. We may doubt whether all we believe is really true, abiding in a state of repressed anger with our questions never resolved. But none of these positions are spiritually healthy. We may exonerate God, but do ourselves harm with an incorrect theological understanding. We may vent our anger by holding God guilty, but destroy our connection with the One who gives meaning and purpose to our humanity. We can stand in doubt and remain susceptible to a deteriorating faith, or, at the least, unpracticed belief.

The "bottom" times of life are crucial; in them we can give ourselves up in despair to deterioration, or we can look for that grace which will enable us to climb from the downside to a new state of well-being. The God who gave us life does not want to hurt us; rather, that Power of grace wants to comfort, heal, and make us whole, bringing us to that completion for which we were created. In that desire God can tolerate our anger and work with our doubt, seeking to strengthen the faith relationship.

I have written this book in an effort to unfold a faith that has a place for anger, that can tolerate doubt, and that can use the bottom times of life as a launch site for a richer and deeper understanding of our existence. It is directed at the anger and confusion that can arise at the time of severe loss. It is written from a Judeo-Christian perspective and its rationality draws upon revelation, which, while it goes beyond empirically provable reasoning, is not necessarily opposed to reason. I hope the reader will find in this book a pathway for the experience of God in the traumatic episode of loss.

In what follows the questions that must be asked will be asked. The questions and the doubts that come with loss will be the vehicles to explore anew the rich faith that God in divine grace holds open to us. In the process, it is my prayer that all of us will emerge renewed, revitalized, and more certain than ever of God's presence with us and abiding love for us.

1
The Experience of Loss

It was sometime in the very early hours of morning; I wasn't really aware of just when. Time was so precious because it was running out. Yet I paid it no attention, hoping, I suppose, that, if I did not mark it, it would somehow be suspended. My son lay in the hospital bed, perspiring profusely in reaction to the heavy doses of narcotics. Breathing was his whole work at the moment. Each breath came in labored gasps because the cancer that was eating voraciously at his body had reached and peppered his lungs.

Just he and I were in the room that night, and between his drugged catnaps we talked. There was so much to say, our hearts were so full, and the time to speak was slipping through our fingers like sand grasped in the hand of a child playing at the beach. But love does not live just through words, and we shared long moments of quiet.

That night words became vessels swollen with meaning; behind each utterance a depth and breadth of feeling not only welled up from the past but also anticipated a future when we would have no more opportunity for expression. Every sound, every gesture, every expression that passed between us was like a floating iceberg; it had a mass beneath it that far exceeded the part that broke the surface.

In that beautiful time of togetherness, I was able to feel and grasp and own forever my son's parting love for me. It came in a short question that in other circumstances would have evoked no more than the import of its query. Those words on this night, however, bespoke a love that focused not on its own desparate circumstances, but on my plight as a father losing his only surviving son—a son who knew he was very loved. The gift came as a last offering of all that was left to give, but it was all that ever really mattered in life at any time. It came wrapped in these velvet words: "Are you upset, Dad?"

Just a few days later, after going into a final coma, my son died of a rare and malicious form of cancer that cut his life short at the age of thirty-five. I would have given myself to that disease without second thought if it would have meant a reprieve for him. But we mortals do not have that kind of control; death is beyond our power. The deepest love of which my humanity was capable could not maintain the breath of life for my son. He was gone from me, and a deep void was left that was as real and as painful as if it had been cut by a surgeon's knife. It was the most profound loss I ever experienced.

What I share here is personal and intimate, but it is, of course, not unique; it is a part of the human journey. Physical death is a part of life, and we will all feel the pangs of its separations. A teenage girl whose father had just died, a father with whom she had lived out a very special relationship, shared her loss with others through these words,

> All people, even the most special person, exist during the
> briefest space in time, so if he is in our past we must accept
> it and begin to rebuild our lives and live with the memories.

The rest of our lives will be more beautiful because our memories of him have colored the windows of our mind; my thoughts are like rainbows. His love for all of us has been painted in colors that will never fade.

Such poignant beauty flowed out of a wound and an emptiness that is common to our humanity, for all of us lose through death people whom we love. In her hurt, this youth saw and expressed what each of us encounters: the briefness of this life, the emptiness we feel because in the death of another we lose a part of ourselves, the irreversible consequence that we must accept, and the necessity to rebuild and go on.

Loss brings us face to face with our own smallness, our own finitude. We humans are not as big as we would like to be; we cannot do all that we would like to do. Nothing so vividly distinguishes us from our Creator and demonstrates that we do not have the wherewithal to be gods of our own lives than the encounter of separation through death. Our life here is but a breath in an infinitesimal moment of the creation that we did not make and cannot control.

In loss also comes the realization of our own aloneness. By *aloneness* I mean that awful experience of our own solitude in which we recognize that, no matter to whom or to what we attach ourselves in this life, the people and things of this world are finite, they have an end point and the attachment will not last forever. Yet, sensing the inherent isolation of our human situation, we reach out to others. Through the process of love, we incorporate them into our own self-system, into what we are. So our sense of identity comes in some degree from our relationships with the significant people in our lives, and we are "so and so's" son, daughter, husband,

wife, father, mother, friend. That is why when we lose someone from our life, we lose a part of ourselves, a piece of our
own identity. And it leaves a hole in us that is very real!

The consequence of loss through death is irreversible; we
cannot put things back in place the way that they were. The
distortion is there, the void is real, the pain comes from a
blow that happened and cannot be taken back. My son is
gone, the father of the teenage girl is also gone; they are only
part of life through memories; we are powerless to change
that reality!

Yet tomorrow is here, life continues, our nature impels us
forward, so we must go on. Grief is that process by which
we rebuild around the void that now exists in ourself. It is
the reconstruction of the self in light of its loss. The altera-
tion does not remove the hole; that will remain as the reality
of all the sharing and caring that will now never take place.
But the rebuilding provides a repair that soothes the pain,
mends the wound, and allows us to function in all the ave-
nues of life that remain open to us. In the aftermath of our
shock and tears, through the trauma of depression and perhaps panic, in the expression of our anger and resentment,
in dealing with the sense of guilt that often accompanies a
separation, and in our own ingrained desire to survive, reality
is affirmed and hope resurfaces. Time does not heal; it is what
takes place in the space that time allows that brings healing.

Loss is a time, then, when we need all the uplifting resources that are a part of our life. But, ironically, loss is also
a time that may shake and attack some of those resources
even if they are a part of our roots.

In the mid sixties my sister lost a very dear friend to
leukemia. The woman was young, in her mid thirties, and a

beautiful person. Her physical comeliness was matched by the inner loveliness of a life that was right with God—the peace and wholeness which the Hebrews call *shalom*. This young, attractive Christian's death was a blow to all who knew her. Her mother, as might be expected, took her loss particularly hard. In fact, she, who herself had been a devoted churchwoman all of her life, left the community of God's people because of the death of her daughter.

She blamed God for her loss. She had prayed that God would spare the life of her lovely child. When the doctors could no longer hold out any medical hope for her, she prayed to Jesus for a miracle. But the miracle that she asked for did not happen, the intervention in the natural life processes that she wanted did not occur; the daughter died. In her anger, the mother turned her back on the God she had worshiped all of her life.

When we need it most, loss can shake the core of our faith even when it has been a part of our roots. As firm a believer as we may be, in the time of loss we cannot hold back the questions that well up within us. We may not vocalize them because most of us are really very hesitant to be angry with a God whom we believe controls our own life and death, but we cannot prevent them from coming into our thoughts. *Why does it have to be this way, Lord? Why my job, God? Why my marriage, Jesus? Why this time of his (or her) life? You said, "Whatever you ask in prayer, you will receive, if you have faith"* (Matt. 21:22), *so why wasn't my prayer granted?*

But faith, if it is sincere, can endure such questions. In fact, faith can survive and grow stronger and more confident. Faith can weather the storms of doubt and come through those emotional low-pressure systems renewed, strengthened, and more secure, finding the sun of God's grace is always shining behind the clouds. Charles Mackintosh observed this truth and wrote, "Faith cannot long keep death in view. Resurrection is that which fills the vision of faith; and in the power thereof, it can rise up from the dead."

Sin lies not in questioning; Jacob wrestled with God (Gen. 32:24-30); Moses argued that he did not have the qualifications for the mission to which God called him (Ex.3:10 to 4:17); Jeremiah lashed out at God for making him a laughingstock among the people (Jer. 20:7-10). Even Jesus of Nazareth prayed in the garden, "My Father, if it be possible let this cup pass from me" (Matt. 26:39). The sin is not in the question; the sin lies in not waiting for the answer! Jacob came out of his bout a different person; Moses survived his argument with God to become an exemplary instrument of divine will; Jeremiah, despite his anger, recognized, "The Lord is with me" (Jer. 20:11). And Jesus, the obedient Son, ended His prayer, "nevertheless, not as I will, but as thou wilt" (Matt. 26:39).

The wrong is not in the doubting; the error lies in the breaking of the relationship. It is like calling someone on the phone, irately chewing him out, and then hanging up without giving him the courtesy of a rebuttal. God made us for relationship, loving relationship with our Creator and with each other through eternity. Love can survive all the honest emotions. In fact, the only way love can survive is through honesty; falsehood never heals.

So the task in loss is not to hold back the doubts that may arise and attack faith; the task is to use that faith to bring forth truth from the ordeal of separation. The work of grief is to rebuild, reviewing the revelations of a Creator who does not want to hurt us but rather cries with us and for us. God wants only to bring us through all the ordeals to that place He has always had in mind for us; God gave us life, not to die, but to live in eternity.

2
Is Anybody Really Out There?

All loss does not occur from the event of physical death. A man whose story came to my attention found himself beset by changes that were drastically altering his life situation. He first lost the woman he had known as his wife, not through death or divorce, but through illness. His wife, in her mid fifties, was diagnosed as a latent schizophrenic; her personality and habits underwent dramatic changes so that she was no longer the same person he had married. Soon after that his son changed jobs and moved halfway across the country. On top of all that change, the man's own job situation was in flux: His company was moving to another state. His options were to move with the company and be some distance from the rest of his family or find a new job. The man sought counseling because of his constant state of anxiety. The anxiety no doubt arose from a feeling that his life was out of control. Such panic is often a part of the grief we experience over the losses that life deals out to each one of us.

Grief is really a process of rehabilitation; it is a rebuilding of ourselves around the privation we have suffered. The work of grief is a lonely work; it can be done only by the person who has experienced the loss. In the death of my son, the loneliness was attested by the friends and relatives who came to me, sought to console me, and invariably said, "I wish that there was something that I could do; I feel so helpless." In their love and concern, they would have done whatever they could to help fill my emptiness, to take away my hurt, and to alleviate the pain I felt. But no one can restructure another individual's self-system around the void of loss; no one can regroup the elements of personal identity after the death of a loved one other than the one who has suffered the separation. In the midst of all those who love us and gather about us to uphold us, we must complete the tasks of grief alone.

After a loss, we feel alone and lonely, perhaps even to the point of wondering about God's reality and presence with us. After the shock, in the midst of the panic, insecurity, depression, anger, and guilt that loss evokes, there seems to be a numbness in which even our Lord is absent. And is not that lack of divine presence validated by the fact that our prayers for healing and survival appeared not to have been heard? We prayed and prayed for the divine touch that could have healed and restored or altered life's events in a more favorable way, but there was only silence.

Is faith just a deception, a psychological ploy that we use to help us handle the mysteries of life? Is the agnostic answer, "We just don't know," the more honest and sensible position? Or is the atheist even more correct in his or her blatant denial, "There is no God"? If we are honest with ourselves, we must admit that in severe loss the question *Is anybody really out there?* surfaces at least in the mind.

A woman who was in the early days of grief over the death of a son said to me, "I can't pray, Pastor. I want to believe; I need to believe that there is more to life than just this. But when I pray, it is as if I am simply talking to the four walls; I feel alone and foolish." The woman could not pray because she was not convinced that there was anyone to hear and we all feel foolish talking to ourselves. Despite her uncertainty, she expressed a desire to believe, even a need to believe. Death had brought her to one of those moments when life moves beyond the limits of what human beings control. If beyond those limits no one were in charge, what hope had she? So she wanted to believe, even needed to believe.

Beyond the limits of the finite where human control cannot go, is there really a Supreme Life, a Being who holds everything in His grasp? Is there a Being who has no limits of control because, having made it all, that Creator has dominion over it all? Our search for reassurance can begin with the reality of our own life, for what is more tangible and real to each of us than the fact of our own being? Life for us begins as infants who come into the world recognizing no boundaries, no distinctions, no separation; there is good indirect evidence that as babies we each perceive that we are everything, everything is us! We come into the world with the perception that we *are* the world!

From the earliest months of life, however, experience begins to bring a more realistic and humbling concept of things. As we go through our days we soon begin to learn that we are not so big, that we share the world with other people and other things. Gradually we apprehend and put into place those boundaries that have to do with the development of our self as an entity that is separate and individual.

The first differentiations are physical and through them we learn the limits of our body—the walls, the crib, and the mobile hanging above are not "us." Later refinements distinguish our will from that of our parents. And, so, the learning continues. By adolescence we know we are not omnipotent, that we can control some aspects of our environment and life but that we have no command over other parts. As individuals we learn that we are free to pursue our own objectives within the bounds of that which we cannot direct. We learn, too, that we are limited not only by physical and psychic confines but also by time: We are encompassed by the frame of our own birth and death.

In this expanding awareness, we come to realize that the knowable reality in which we exist and operate is but a small part of something immensely larger. As we build more and more powerful telescopes and probe further and further with our space technology, we are able to discern planets and stars associated in galaxies, the number and extent of which we have no definitive knowledge; we never see the end, we are unable to count it all. But just as we have learned how to look farther out, we have also developed technology that enables us to look deeper within. As we have done so, the atom, once thought to be the smallest unit of matter, exploded before the eyes of science into a teeming reality of wildly traveling electrons. In this subatomic world, we have found insights that provide a fuller understanding of the basic force fields of nature.

All of this is part of a system which Albert Einstein explained as a four-dimensional space-time continuum that turns back upon itself and has no beginning and no end. There is a relatedness about it all. One scientist wrote, "But in its vast cosmic picture, when fully revealed, the abyss between macrocosmos and microcosmos—the very big and the very little—will surely be bridged, and the whole complex of the universe will resolve into a homogeneous fabric."[1]

Confronted with the fact of this cosmos, you and I who come into the world thinking that we *are* the world grow to understand our smallness and our impermanence. The boundaries which we gradually apprehend and which set each of us apart as an independent individual are limiting; they mark us off but they also confine us and diminish us. The realization that was noted in the opening chapter surfaces: We are not as big as we would like to be; we cannot do all that we would like to do! Behind those boundaries and under the awareness of our own mortality, we gradually come to experience the implications of our solitude.

As we grow older the knowledge of our "apartness" becomes an awful sense of our aloneness; it generates a pain of isolation. In the words of Gale Webbe, "Man is a lonely creature at best. The history of the world can most tellingly be read as the story of man's efforts to escape his loneliness, even as the history of religion is essentially the story of what God does about man's aloneness."[2]

Aloneness is different than loneliness. To be lonely is to be without company, a condition that can be rectified by seeking out and joining with others. Aloneness is that terrible appreciation of our own separateness which must admit to its ultimate solitariness. It is that understanding that we can never link with another human being in such a way that either life could be lengthened by the joining. Essentially we stand alone facing the reality of our own physical death.

Perhaps that is why men and women have a natural tendency to reach out to something which is beyond what we see and know here. All known societies have beliefs in a spirit world. In the absence of any more tangible evidence than an intuitive connectedness with something that goes beyond and stands above our humanity, primitive people postulated various deities. These postulations cannot be labeled mere fiction. Out of the sense that we are a part of something that goes beyond our human ability to entirely comprehend, there grows the certainty of an Ultimate Truth by which it all was generated and under which its destiny is guided. The most primitive response to this is the hypothesis of a spirit world.

Somewhere, then, in the deepest recesses of what we are, there exists an untaught awareness that we are not alone; it seems to exist as an inborn correction against the madness that might develop from a sense of complete isolation. It is a primeval sense that in our separateness, amid all the infinite vastness of the cosmos that surrounds us, there is a connectedness. We are an infinitesimal unit within it, yet we are a part of that larger reality, a part of its vastness, its awesomeness, its structural complexity, its magnificent design, its mystery, as well as its purpose. The feeling was put into words by a psychiatric patient toward the end of her therapy. She said, "I don't know how to talk about this thing. I just feel connected, real, like I am a part of a very big picture, and even though I can't see much of the picture, I know it's there and I know it's good and I know I am part of it."[3]

Somewhere in the depths of our nature there is an intuitive knowledge of the unity of the whole, and with this motivation we reach out to touch that which can reveal its significance. We search for Truth, for a Creator in an effort to find the meaning of our own existence.

The search for meaning is a quest for that connection with the Infinite that will extend our own limitedness and perhaps take away that fearful aloneness we know. In that condition of aloneness we are motivated to cling to family, friends, clubs, communities, and nation. We find some relief from our isolation in belonging. But human companionship is not enough, for all such attachments are finite, like ourselves; they are unlasting; they will also die.

So relationship with that which is also mortal cannot

really dispel the fear and anxiety of aloneness. Try as we may, we cannot lose ourselves in preoccupation with our social alliances, our causes, our vacations, the unending parade of toys with which we fill our lives, our accumulation of wealth and even our self-aggrandizement through achieving status or gaining power. The feeling of isolation remains no matter how much of this present world we control. Only a connectedness with the whole of reality, a sense of personal meaningfulness that makes us a part of a continuing purpose can yield legitimate hope. That hope is the only balm for our aloneness; it is the hope we seek from Truth.

Truth has gone by many different names; the gods of humanity are legion. And if men and women had never been able to get beyond just hypothesis, we would have been condemned to remain in the primitive state. We have not remained so because that Truth, of which all known societies have an innate sense and a reasoned conception, has chosen to reveal Himself. The revelation is not a full disclosure, but it is a convincing glimpse. It began with a nomad band of Semite people who were brought out of the enslavement of Egypt some thirteen hundred years before the birth of Christ. They were called Israel; their story begins in the Book of Exodus and unfolds throughout the Old Testament of the Bible. They came to know Truth as Yahweh, the Creator, Redeemer, and Sustainer of life.

Israel's cognizance of the reality of Truth as the one and only God, Sovereign of the universe, did not come about because of any special human faculty they possessed that enabled them to find and identify this Supreme Being. They became aware of God because Yahweh came to them and made the divine self known. Thus Abram was called to leave his home and go to "the land that I will show you" (Gen.

12:1), and Moses was addressed with the words, "I am
. . . the God of Abraham, the God of Isaac, and the God of
Jacob" (Ex. 3:6). The people Israel came to know Yahweh
because Truth came to them in a particular way through
earthly events and opened their awareness to His presence.
Revelation is encounters where the divine and the human
cross paths at God's initiative.

Through Israel's divinely initiated encounter, some people
recognized a fuller and more tangible revelation. The Creator
God took on human flesh and dwelt among the people on
earth in the form of Jesus of Nazareth. The prophets,
through whom God had spoken in the past, were simply
human instruments revealing God's presence and will. For
those of faith, Jesus Christ spoke not *for* God but *as* God.
"[He] dwelt among us, full of grace and truth" (John 1:14).
Truth became a living, speaking Word for those who listened, who learned, and who joined in the relationship.

So the evidence from our intuitive nature and humanity's
experience with revelation that breaks into human history is
that Somebody really is "out there." Our sense of connectedness with the Creator became concrete in the experiences of
Abraham, Moses, a people called Israel, the disciples of Jesus
of Nazareth, Saul (Paul) of Tarsus, and hosts of others. It is
the reality behind the statement, "I want to believe," made
by the woman who said she could not pray. It is the reality
that keeps those of us who do pray from feeling alone and
foolish.

In grief we can close ourself off, retreat into ourselves as
a kind of reflexive defense mechanism and, thus, cut the
connections even with God. The validity for our disconnect-
ing tends to be reinforced if we feel that God didn't come
through on the promises made to us—our loss was not avert-

ed. In this state we can generate the illusion: I cannot hear God or feel the Divine; therefore, the Almighty really isn't there—or, if there, really isn't listening. In the next two chapters we will explore an explanation of God's presence not only "out there" but *with* us and *in* each one of us. Further, we shall see that it is an abiding presence in faithfulness to the promise, "Lo, I am with you always" (Matt. 28:20). But, alas, it is a Presence that by our own cognitive devices we can exclude from our lives.

3
Are You Really Down Here Too?

The following words are recorded in the Book of Moses called Exodus.

> There the angel of the Lord appeared to him in flames of fire from within a bush. Moses saw that though the bush was on fire it did not burn up. So Moses thought, "I will go over and see this strange sight—why the bush does not burn up." When the Lord saw that he had gone over to look, God called to him from within the bush, "Moses, Moses!" . . . . "I am the God of your father, the God of Abraham, the God of Isaac and the God of Jacob." At this, Moses hid his face, because he was afraid to look at God (Ex. 3:2-6, NIV).

That incident is dated sometime about thirteen hundred years before the birth of Christ. Now read a description of a similar event closer in time.

> Suddenly I heard a deep voice speak directly into my ear. "What—what did you say?" I whirled around to find no one behind me. There was the voice again: "Tonight you must make a decision for me. If you don't, it will be too late." I shook my head and said automatically: "Why?" (The reply came) "It just will be!" Was I losing my marbles? It was God and he knew me![1]

Those are the words of Merlin Carothers, a man who went
from a prison cell to become a Methodist minister and founder of the Foundation of Praise. He wrote them sometime
prior to 1970.

One evening I personally experienced the presence of God
in a different way. There was no apparition, and I heard no
voice, but it was as real to me as if I had experienced such
phenomena. God's presence that night took the form of a
calming influence that brought a release from anxiety. For
several months I had been laboring under the burden of
business losses that continued to mount. Then my wife had
to be hospitalized for an extended period, the outcome of
which was not absolutely predictable. I came home from a
hospital visit one night weary from a long day, anxious over
my wife's condition and the state of my business circumstances, feeling I could carry this load no further. In the dark
loneliness of that empty house, I dropped to my knees to cry
out for help. In that prayer I poured out my helplessness, my
unworthiness, and my need. I told Jesus I wanted to take
advantage of His gracious offer, "Come to me, all you who
are weary and burdened, and I will give you rest" (Matt.
11:28,NIV). I wanted and needed a rest that I could not find
or create for myself. I surrendered myself to Christ's will for
my life and pledged that each day, one day at a time, if He
would open the doors I should go through, I would with all
my human power endeavor to go through them.

When I got up from that prayer, I felt an immediate sense
of release. I went to bed and slept a deep, refreshing sleep
such as I had not had for many weeks. In the morning the
problems were all still there, but I was able to face them with
a newfound energy and confidence. In six months I was able
to look back on a period that saw my wife's release from the

hospital with a new capability to function normally and a financial situation that was surely making a recovery. It all began on a night that God heard my distress and granted a promise that was already a reality awaiting my surrender.

My experience was much like an incident reported by John Wesley, the founder of Methodism. He wrote, "After my return home, I was much buffeted with temptations; but cried out, and they fled away. They returned again and again. I as often lifted up my eyes, and he 'sent me help from his holy place.' "

People have experienced the presence of the Creator-God in their lives in many ways throughout history. Israel, as it was being molded into a self-conscious people during the forty-year trek through the Sinai, perceived God going before them "by day . . . in a pillar of cloud to guide them on their way and by night in a pillar of fire to give them light" (Ex. 13:21, NIV). The writings of the prophets and the apostles provide a record of a variety of personal confrontations with the One in whose power the universe resides. The Book of Psalms is a poetic outpouring of the inner human experience of a God who is not only Creator and Judge but also Sustainer and Redeemer.

Where does this Power lodge itself? The first Hebrews who came to the Canaanite country from Mesopotamia conceived their God as residing on the peaks of the earth which were closest to the heavens. He was El Shaddai, the Mountain One, and early Scripture refers frequently to "the mountain of God" (Ex. 3:1). During the wanderings of the Hebrews through the wilderness of the Sinai, a special tent pitched outside the bounds of the camp was where Moses met with God. It was appropriately known as "the tent of meeting" and the Divine Presence when it came there was marked by a pillar of cloud at its entrance (Ex. 33:9). Later, when the Israelites took up residence in Canaan, a more permanent tent known as "the tabernacle of the congregation" was erected. In Jewish belief this tent became the abode of God's presence with them. Finally, under King Solomon a magnificent building, the Temple, was built that contained an area known as the holy of holies. It was in this area that Israel then believed God's presence on earth to be.

Even though God was envisioned as having a residing place on earth, since the earliest times of the Judeo-Christian tradition, believers have understood that the Creator cannot be "contained"; God is always "Lord of heaven and earth." When God acts it is from "out of heaven" (Gen. 19:24). God is far off in a heaven, which has no bounds, and God is near on an earth, which does have limits. Seneca, a Roman philosopher of the first century, expressed this idea: "Nothing is void of God; He Himself fills His work." Although the Creator's seat or throne was always understood to be in heaven, the Divine Presence also was believed to dwell among humanity (Ex. 25:8).

That experience of God's presence has been more personal than just a residence on a mountain or in a tent or within some other holy place on earth; it is also an inner presence experienced by the believer. "For thus says the high and lofty One who inhabits eternity, whose name is Holy: 'I dwell in the high and holy place, and also with him who is of a contrite and humble spirit' " (Isa. 57:15).

The covenant promise, "I will put my law within them, and I will write it upon their hearts; and I will be their God and they shall be my people" (Jer. 31:33), bespeaks a relationship which is internal and intimate. That is a covenant reflected in the words of Jesus, "Remain in me, and I will remain in you" (John 15:4, NIV). The New Testament describes the relationship: "No one has ever seen God; but if we love each other, God lives in us and his love is made complete in us" (1 John 4:12, NIV). The experience of the people of faith is that our Creator dwells not only "with us" but also as a part of us—that is, "within us."

Augustine applied logic to understand this truth. I have paraphrased his questions: Is there anything in me that can contain you; indeed, can the heaven or earth which you have made contain you? Or as nothing can exist without you who made it all, doesn't whatever exists contain you? Why should I ask then, that you come into me, since I indeed exist and could not exist if you were not in me. I could not exist, could not exist at all, unless you *were* in me.[2] But how can God be in us, in each one of us?

Before we go further, I must state that the answer we seek will not be associated with the realm of magic. It is necessary to make this distinction because, when we think about the processes of God, we often tend to ascribe them to some kind of magical means. Since a mystery is involved in spiritual realities, consigning them to a magical process may seem legitimate. For example, prayer can be understood as a prodigious communication by which thought-messages fly through the ether and are somehow absorbed by a God who is "out there" always ready to receive. Our human petitions, once heard by this Being, are either responded to with appropriate divine manipulations of natural phenomena to grant the request or, for whatever reason, are ignored and go unanswered. This is a childlike conception in which God is seen as the great Parent/King who responds to us in magical ways that alter natural processes and, thus, produce effects upon our lives. Many adults understand prayer this way.

When our faith does not mature, our religious understandings remain at the level of childhood thinking. Contrary to the magical ideas of immature reason, God works through the ordinary. After all, the Creator established reality as a fully functioning system. The day-to-day processes are meant to provide the means by which we are to exist with our Maker. As Gale Webbe pointed out, "The extraordinary, the occasional, the extrasensory, are not in the slightest degree the essential data of mature personal religion."[3] The visions, the miracles—and they do occur—are simply the momentary discernment of eternal reality that has broken into time. The *how* and the *why* are mysteries, but the breakthrough is simply the evidence that there is more to God's reality than we see and comprehend here and now.

Henri Nouwen has described with simplicity and clarity the movement necessary to grow from magical ideas of religion to mature faith.[4] A mature religious faith is a matter of developing particular attributes. Nouwen explains that this mature faith resides in a flexible religion, able to "integrate all new knowledge within its frame of reference and keep pace with all the new discoveries of the human mind."[5] From such a perspective, we will seek to answer the question previously posed: How is it possible for God to be in each one of us?

In the very clever book *The Screwtape Letters,* C. S. Lewis captured a great deal of insight about the human condition. He put those gems into the letters of one of Satan's ministers, Screwtape, who is attempting to teach his nephew how to ensnare human beings for the devil's cause. In one of those letters Screwtape explains to his nephew, "As spirits they (human beings) belong to the eternal world, but as animals they inhabit time."[6] It is often very hard for us human beings to see the truth of that statement concerning our nature, but we do belong to two realms. Being "in time," that is living a temporal existence, the here and now is very real and vivid to us. But many persons are not convinced that there is also an eternal aspect to our nature. Such doubts or denials can be readily seen in the way so many people go blithely through life, giving no mind to that aspect of their humanity. We live for today, unmindful that God created each one of us to live in eternity. We shall take a closer look at certain aspects of our humanity in order to see (1) that we are designed and meant to live not only in this present existence on earth but also beyond this life and (2) that God really does live in us.

When we ask with the psalmist, "What is man?" the most obvious answer is that we are a living physical body; we first use our physical reality to identify us as a unique being. As we develop through infancy, the first distinctions that we make that delineate our "self" from other things and people are made on the basis of our bodies. We learn that the rungs of the crib and the ceiling in the room are not us, that there are tangible limits that mark off what we are. The infant's early learning revolves around the discovery of its body; its parts, what each can do, and what together they can produce and accomplish. Our body is the first reality which we identify as "me."

The body is conceived in the mating process, it differentiates in the womb, it is deposited into the world at birth, it grows to maturity, but, eventually, for one reason or another, it ceases to function and dies. So the body is finite; it has a beginning, a certain existence, and comes to an end. If all we are is a body, we are finite and nothing more. That's a depressing thought from which we run. We live each day with the knowledge of our own physical demise, even if we do try to repress the thought and ignore for as long as we can the death that lies ahead.

But the good news (which is the meaning of the word *gospel*) is that this depressing thought arises out of our own shortsightedness, our own denial of our full humanity. Our nature *is* more than a physical body which will die. The God who designed the creation for eternal relationship could not be involved in the destruction of this divine purpose. If we, God's creatures, were destined for death, it would be a divine self-violation, a contradiction of the whole intent of the creative work; it would be a "house divided against itself." Our Creator is the God of the living, not of the dead (Mark 12:27). The built-in rescinding of that loving act which gave life would make no more rational sense than it would be for loving human parents to contemplate at birth the annihilation of their own children. Could God, who is the very definition of love (1 John 4:8) be less loving than the best human being who is made in His image?

How then are we to understand this immortal aspect of ourselves which is different from the physical body which does die? The Greek philosophers recognized these two aspects of our humanity by dividing what we are into two parts, the body and the soul. The soul was believed to be both preexistent and immortal. But the Hebrews did not conceive of such a separation; to the Hebrew a person was one "living" entity—the soul did not exist apart from the body. Soul, for the ancient Jew, was the "aliveness" of the body, apparent in the whole range of feelings which affect a state of mind.

This is very similar to the way in which the "human spirit" has been understood in the Christian church: the person in the fullness of his or her powers as a living, active being.

Reference to the human spirit has been a way of characterizing the fact that life, soul, or will and mind exist integrally to what we are as human beings. Just as the Spirit of God is a characterization of God as a person (not something which exists outside of or next to God), the human spirit describes the "aliveness" of the person which each of us are.

This "aliveness," then, is the part of us that does not die, the part to which we refer when we speak of our "life" or our "soul." It is that which comes from the Creator of life and empowers our being (Gen. 2:7). In our present existence, this "aliveness" is housed in a physical body, but it is not extinguished when the physical dies. This present "tent" of flesh is eventually put away, after which we live on in an everlasting housing provided by God (2 Cor. 5:1,NIV).

The apostle Paul likened the process by which our "aliveness," our soul, makes this transition to the growth of a seed into the fullness of the plant. The thing which is sown, the flesh, is perishable; what is raised is imperishable. The body in which the soul has resided, through its physical death gives rise to the completeness of the spirit, that is, the fullness of our empowerment for life. What can that be but the eternal life our Creator has fashioned us for? Paul then restated his case in this way:

> Flesh and blood cannot inherit the kingdom of God, nor does the perishable inherit the imperishable. Listen, I tell you a mystery: We will not all sleep, but we will all be changed . . . For the trumpet will sound, and the dead will be raised imperishable, and we will be changed. For the perishable must clothe itself with the imperishable and the mortal with immortality (1 Cor. 15:50-53, NIV).

The soul is our word for the living power breathed into us by God at life's inception which is meant to exist eternally.

Part of what this gift of "aliveness" powers is the functioning of the mind. Our mind conceives who we are, it is the place of that being whom we identify as "self." The mind not only thinks and makes decisions for us, it is us! This "self" incorporates the body in its image because we cannot conceive ourselves without our physical parts, but we know that the body alone, by itself, is not "us."

The mind is also the willful part of our being; it is the part through which the freedom we have been granted by our Creator becomes functional. The state of mind controls, determines, what the body will do. As the seat of the "self," the mind plots out the course that our life will follow. From our mind springs the "will" that we exhibit. The freedom of that will is an essential aspect of our humanity.

The human mind is, we've come to know, a very complicated and intriguing mechanism. What we know about it is infinitesimal compared with what we don't know. We can identify two parts of it through inference. That is, through experiencing how our mind operates, we know that there is a conscious aspect where we are in control, but that there is also a part we cannot direct, which exerts a directing and controlling influence upon us. This "unconscious" part of our mind, psychology now knows, is by far the larger portion. It is not possible to measure either the conscious or the unconscious, but those who work with these realities say that probably 5 percent of the mind is associated with our conscious functioning, while the unconscious constitutes the other 95 percent. Jung has likened it to an iceberg, the conscious being the smaller part which we can see above the surface, while the great bulk, the unconscious, rides out of sight below the dark waters. The next chapter will suggest that this unconscious is even more vast than many have ever believed it to be.

Everyone of those parts, body, soul, and mind is real and functional. To deny any component is to deny our own humanity and, thereby, to forfeit the fullest development of what we were created to be. By refusing to recognize the eternal nature of our being, the soul, we doom ourselves to live each day with the specter of eventual death.

But we have not yet finished with the matter, for we must now explore how God feeds into what we are and becomes a real power within us. We must see where a connection comes into play and how that may possibly operate. The next chapter will propose a way in which God is very literally "in us."

4
But How Are We Connected?

"How do you know after you have prayed for God's help that the decisions you then make and the actions you then take are not simply the choices and desires of your own will?" That was the question that Reggie (a fictitious name to disguise identity) put to me as we talked together in my study. The man was forty years old and had just recently been separated from his wife of nineteen years and his four children. When he had come to me for help, he exhibited all the signs of separation distress: intense discomfort, depression, anxiety, and panic. Since Reggie was a person of faith, my initial effort in counseling was to help him recover his sense of God's presence. This would help him gain the assurance needed to face the many problems that were presently a part of his life. We had talked about prayer as a channel through which God's power and guidance become accessible at the operational level of our own living. But how this was a realistic possibility was not at all clear to Reggie at the moment, and he raised his question with me.

Reggie's question reflects an uncertainty that may arise in all episodes of separation, whether the loss be through divorce, dismissal from a job, a financial setback, a health problem, or the death of a loved one. When out of a sense of our helplessness we pray, "Lord, guide me each day, one day at a time, to do those things and make those decisions that will bring relief and recovery," how do we know with any certainty that our subsequent decisions and acts are not simply the choices and desires of our own will? Can God intervene in our lives in some nonmagical way that affects the daily events of our living? As we begin our search for an answer to that question consider the following true accounts.

After it was all over Teresa Apgar wondered, "Was it fate?" She had turned south, heading away from her destination, on a road with which she was thoroughly familiar, having no intention whatever to do so. But as a result of that turn she was positioned to save the life of a truck driver who would have otherwise perished in the explosion of his wrecked tank truck.[1]

Merlin Carothers tells the story of an army major who was miraculously rescued from capture during the Vietnam war. The major had been seriously wounded so that he could not escape the enemy who were closing in to take prisoners. As part of this account Carothers tells what was reported by the rescuing helicopter pilot as he was flying north.

> He felt a sudden overpowering urge to turn and go east. *But why?* he reasoned. His destination was north. Contrary to all military rules he made a ninety-degree turn and headed east. He felt an even stronger urge to fly lower and slower. This was even less logical than his first urge and contrary to all rules of flying over hostile territory.[2]

Armando Valladares was a political prisoner held in Cuban prisons for twenty-two years. In his book *Against All Hope: The Prison Memoirs of Armando Valladares,* he gave a detailed and irrefutable description of the starvation, torture, and threats of death that he suffered over the years.[3] When the pain, fear, and lack of sleep began seriously to affect him, he sought God and asked for the spiritual strength to endure those conditions. He then wrote, "And his presence, which I felt, made my faith an indestructible shield."

Does God have such an immediate access to our life that divine influence can turn us south on a road when our destination lies north; or provoke us to take risks that endanger our own life in order to rescue another; or infuse us with the power to bear an ordeal which has the potential to emotionally devastate us? But that is really not the right question to ask. The evidence from human experience is that this does happen and happens to a degree where coincidence is statistically untenable. So the question should not be, "Does it happen?" but, "How is it possible?" Is there something in the reality of our humanity, something in the way we are constituted, that provides a mysterious connection with our Creator? We have acquired enough insight about the workings of the human psyche to make it possible to project a very tenable answer to that question.

Psychology teaches that one of the definitive characteristics of our self-identity is our sense of being in relationship. One of the definitive characteristics of our humanity is our sense of relationship with the Being who gave us life. For those of faith the characteristic is embedded in the understanding "in the image of God he created him, male and female he created them" (Gen.1:27). This reference does not mean that you and I look like God or that there are faculties in our nature that can be identified with those of God. Rather, it refers to the fact that the Creator willed a creature in the divine image who could love and be loved as God does.

The image that God casts originates from a nature which is the prototype of love (1 John 4:8). People were created for relationship with God and each other; being in the image of the divine, love is to be the character of that association.

What are the mechanisms of this loving relationship; how can the association with God transpire? There is a mystery to all of this that we can never fully explain, but there is an aspect of our humanity that can function as an open link with our Creator; it exists in a component of our mind. A great deal of the knowledge we have about our mind and how it works comes through the field of psychiatry. As clinical scientists have probed the mental processes, they have confirmed that the human mind has various levels which function interrelatedly. They have also become aware that through our mind we are somehow connected with universal material and notions that go beyond what we have consciously and purposively come by. What has been learned now enables us to conceptualize how it is possible for God to be with us and in us constantly. The processes by which this happens are mysterious but operate through the ordinary in extraordinary ways. They do not rule out, but at the same time do not depend upon, the miraculous. They are certainly not magical. The insights we have began to open to us through the study of dreams.

Sigmund Freud, the father of modern psychiatry, opened the study of the unconscious in concert with his investigation of dreams. In 1900 he published *The Interpretation of Dreams,* a landmark study based on his work. Freud demonstrated a technique by which the significance of dreams could be explored and developed in light of a person's life situation. His studies also showed that there is a connection between the unconscious and the conscious activity of our mind. This connection, he explained, can legitimately be analyzed and that from studying the processes that underlie the dream we can come to an understanding of the forces that work in the mind.

Others tested his theories, found his conclusions valid and his methods effective, and went on to elaborate his pioneering efforts. Carl Jung was one of those people and in the course of a half century of psychiatric work with patients analyzed some eighty thousand dreams. There is not space here, nor is it my intent, to present even an overview of Jung's investigations. What I do want to note are some of the findings Jung emerged with as the result of forty-five years of research and clinical experience. An excellent, concise summary of these can be found in Wayne Rollins' book *Jung and the Bible*.[4]

Jung learned that our dreams are like hidden doors into the innermost recesses of our soul. Some reveal insights about a person's hidden problems or guarded secret, some seem to preview coming events in the dreamer's future, others can reveal answers to a current problem or provide a creative new idea. But one of the most amazing discoveries was that there is a universality in the content of some dreams that surmounts both time and culture—dreams sometimes contain material that we ourselves never learned or experienced firsthand that comes from other times and foreign places.

From his studies Jung formulated an understanding of the unconscious part of our mind that was two dimensional. It was composed of what he called the *personal unconscious* which contains material relating closely to one's personal life, such as ideas and impressions temporarily lost to memory and thoughts too objectional to the conscious mind to be acknowledged. A second, deeper layer of the mind he called the *collective unconscious* which contained material associated with universal human experience that went beyond anything we might have been directly associated with in our own time or own culture.

Jung also found that there was communication between the conscious and the unconscious areas of the mind. Dreams are one vehicle for such exchange, but there were others that also operated during wakefulness: the "Freudian slip" of tongue or behavior; whims; the prodding we feel from our conscience; the encounter of serendipity which opens up new potentials; even the development of a neurotic condition or experiencing deep-seated fears, anxieties, and depression which alert us to a malfunction in our mental development or behavior. All of these and many more are examples of the influence of the unconscious on our conscious life.

The deeper layer of our mind, Jung discovered, functions in a balancing and compensatory way to maintain our health and growth. In other words, if we consciously discard or ignore things that are vital to the maintenance of our life and growth, such that they completely disappear from awareness, the unconscious will develop a compensating counteraction to the jeopardizing behavior. This will then be present, subtly influencing self-preserving tendencies. Thus the impetus of the unconscious in its influence is always to guide and empower the positive development of the self which resides in the conscious. The communications we receive from it, then, are always for the purpose of propelling us toward honesty, truthfulness, and reality.

The vehicle through which this principle operates is the ordinary—the dreams, slips, whims, conscience, flashes of insight, neurotic symptomatology, and so forth. But the ordinary can contain an extraordinary dimension when recognized, attended to, and acted upon: "Who would have ever thought . . .?" "I never would have believed . . .," "It was absolutely amazing!" Again, it is appropriate to emphasize: God designed life to operate through the ordinary and natural processes which the Creator built into the master design. The miracle happens, but not routinely!

At this point, if we have not already done so, we must begin to wonder about the source of these things that become available to us through the unconscious—the heritage; wisdom; orientation toward health and growth; espousal of honesty, truth, and reality as the only perspectives from which to operate; the warning of uncomfortableness; the balancing and compensating for our own self-destructive tendencies; the urge to become more than we are. What "mind" generates such things if they do not arise within our own consciousness? How is this part of our humanity connected with all humanity over time and across space: cultures which are personally unknown to us, intelligence that cannot be accounted for by our own learning or experience? And from whence does its interest in the preservation and development of "our" self arise, if it does not originate through that "self" which is lodged in our consciousness and which we know as "me"?

There can be only one such Source; it must lie in the Eternal, the Omniscient; it must be both Alpha and Omega, Beginning and End. From it must spring the Font of Truth, Love and Knowledge. It must be the Root of the Plant and the Vine which produces the fruit. It is the Ultimate Proponent of Life, its Author and Sustainer. It can be none other than the Creator of it all, the One whom we call God!

There is no other entity whom we could name or propose

who could qualify logically because nothing known to us
except the power we apprehend as Almighty God could
fulfill what this Source must be. It must be transcendent
Spirit existing beyond time and the universe; yet it must be
condescendent Presence residing *with* us and *in* each one of
us. It must be cognizant of all history; but it must exceed that
history, be outside of it. Such a Source must be the epitome
of faithful self-giving in its unswerving bent to protect and
promote life by endlessly battling the force of Evil that seeks
to destroy and kill life. It must be the wellspring of wholeness
as it empowers its creatures to become what they were always, from the beginning, meant to be. The character of that
Source must be *love;* and its operational mode must be *grace.*

Now all this operational reality is quite unprovable by our
science, but it is not necessarily at variance with that science.
Scott Peck is a physician and psychiatrist who, in his book
The Road Less Traveled, linked his understanding as a scientist with his revelational insights as a Christian. From that
stance he explained that to account for this miraculous force
of grace that operates in our life we hypothesize the existence
of a God that loves us and wants us to grow. He then commented,

> To many this hypothesis seems too simple, too easy; too
> much like fantasy; childlike and naive. But what else do we
> have? To ignore the data by using tunnel vision is not an
> answer. We cannot obtain an answer by not asking the ques-
> tions. Simple though it may be, no one who has observed the
> data and asked the questions has been able to produce a
> better hypothesis or even really a hypothesis at all. Until
> someone does, we are stuck with this strangely childlike
> notion of a loving God or else with a theoretical vacuum.[5]

All that we have discussed points to God as the source of the power of life. We have now seen how that Source can be made available to us through the mystery of our unconscious, functioning as an avenue by which the Creator who made us is even now *with us* and *in us,* sustaining the original gift and seeking its fulfilment. Notice too that I have said "an" avenue, for the power and mystery of God can never be proscribed. What has been characterized is a channel by which we are joined to that which Peck has described as "a powerful force originating outside of human consciousness which nurtures the spiritual growth of human beings."[6]

Thus we can see that in the episode of our loss, as well as in all the other experiences of life, there is Someone "out there." And not only "out there" as a distant Deity who has created life from which the Creator then remains separate as would an observer, but is "with us" and "in us" as One who is a functional part of the life that has been brought into being.

Finally we are now in a position to offer a response to Reggie's question which opened this chapter: "How do you know after you have prayed for God's help that the decisions you then make and the actions you then take are not simply the choices and desires of your own will?" The answer lies in the understanding of surrender.

Through the surrender of our will to God's direction, we actualize the vital channel of communication described in this chapter. That surrender, growing out of a recognition of our own helplessness, allows God's wisdom and guidance to emerge in the thoughts and ideas that enter our consciousness. If we believe that God exists and the evidence presented in this chapter that the impetus of the unconscious is always to guide and empower positive development, we cannot help but acknowledge that in an attitude of surrender, by definition, we are in that state of mind whereby we are allowing God's influence to permeate our being. If we are not playing games, that is pretending to surrender in an attempt to manipulate God, but are honestly yielding ourselves completely, the conscious part of our mind is open to receive all the benefits of that amazing grace. The experience of Raul Ries demonstrates what surrender is and to what it can lead.

Raul is the pastor of a church in California, but his background would never lead you to believe that he would become a minister. Raul was the product of an unhappy childhood home. He admits that he hated his father and that he was full of anger. He vented that anger by becoming a tough guy. He studied and practiced the martial arts, and his interests revolved around fighting. When he was eighteen years old he beat a man so severely that the man almost died. He was arrested and, when judged guilty, was given the choice of either going to fight in Vietnam or being sentenced to a jail term. He choose to join the Marines, but even there he continued to get into trouble. He underwent psychiatric treatment and was eventually given an honorable discharge.

Raul married after his discharge, but the marriage was not a loving relationship. He vented his pent-up anger that he carried around from his childhood on his wife. He would, he admits, actually beat her. He opened a martial arts school which grew quite successfully, but he said, "I still felt empty." He sought release from his inner tensions through promiscuous sexual relations and through fighting. Raul tells of how his wife would try to talk to him about God, but he always refused to listen. Finally, tired of the beatings, the infidelity, and all the fighting, his wife announced that she was going to leave him the next day and take the children with her. That night she went to her Bible study as usual.

While she was gone, the anger in Raul mounted until he became desparate and irrational. He decided that when she returned he would kill her and their two children and then himself. But, in that agitated state, a strange thing happened. Raul says, "I heard a voice say, 'Accept me today or you never will.'" For some reason he then turned on the TV, and a minister was talking about how God is the only one who could save us.

Surrender came. In Raul's own words this is what happened. "I felt my anger break inside of me. I knelt down in our living room and cried for the first time in years. That is when the Holy Spirit touched me and I accepted Christ into my heart. I have never looked back."

Allowing God's will to permeate his thoughts and actions, Raul was led into the ordained ministry. On any given Sunday, Pastor Ries leads the worship of five thousand people in Calvary Chapel in West Covina—an old supermarket converted into a church to accommodate his rapidly growing ministry.[7]

From what has been presented, we can see the crucial position that our human will occupies. The conscious, which is the willful part of our mind directly under our control, can cooperatively open our life through surrender to God to use all that is fed to it, or it can ignore and turn away from that opportunity. The experience of loss is a time when we may be sorely tempted to turn away from God. For if God is not only "out there" but also "with us" and "in us" here on earth, if this Creator has made us for relationship which is to be loving in nature, then why was my prayer for healing or help not granted? Why does God whose nature is "love" say no to us? It is to this question that we turn in the next chapter.

5
Then Why Did You Say No?

When my son's cancer was diagnosed as synovial cell sarcoma, the specialists at Sloan-Kettering knew they were dealing with a rare and very malicious form of the disease for which surgery was the only treatment available. The only hope they could extend then was to amputate the leg in which the tumor had appeared in the hope that the cancer had not spread and would, thus, be eliminated. I immediately asked God, over and over, to please let it be contained and removed by the amputation.

Seven months later I knew that those prayers had not been granted; there were now five spots of the disease in the lungs. The only treatment again was surgical removal. My prayers continued to be, "Please, Lord, this time let it be contained and, thus, removed by the surgery."

Within weeks, I realized that this prayer also was not to be granted; the cancer was discovered in the back, in the abdomen, and probably was in other places. Medically there was no more hope; no human being could save the life of my son from this awful disease. We needed a miracle, and that was my next prayer.

I thought of all the healings that Jesus performed while He lived among the people of ancient Israel. I searched them out in the Scriptures and reread many of them. Blind Bartimaeus called out to Jesus in Jericho as He was passing by, pleading, "Master, let me receive my sight." Jesus, moved with pity, healed him (Mark 10:46-52). A leper declared his belief in his request, "If you will, you can make me clean." He was cleansed of his affliction (Mark 1:40-45). The Roman centurion, who saw himself as an unworthy sinner, sent to Jesus a request that his faithful servant be healed. The soldier was the "enemy" of the Jews, the conqueror, the foreign occupier. Despite such apparent unworthiness, his request was granted; his servant was healed (Luke 7:1-10). The episodes of healing go on and on in the Gospels.

So I called out to God in my distress. I stated my faith, "I know, Lord, that all power lies in you; you, and you alone, can heal my son." I confessed my unworthiness to ask and acknowledged my sinfulness. I prayed for the miracle, and I hoped God might be moved with pity, as was Jesus by the appeal of Bartimaeus, to rid my son of this malicious evil that was taking his life. But the prayer was not granted; on June 25, 1986, my son died. I could not stem the question that reared up in my mind, for I so wanted that young man to live, *Why did you say no, Lord?*

But I did not feel singled out; God says no to others. King David, a chosen one, received a no when he prayed that his child be healed. David had committed adultery with Bathsheba and then plotted to have her husband killed in battle so that he might marry her. The infant that was the fruit of that illicit union was stricken after his birth, and the king pleaded with God for the life of the child. He kept a strict fast, he slept on the bare ground at night, he covered himself with sackcloth, and he would not eat with the officials of his household. Seven days after the onset of the affliction, the child died; the answer to all of David's supplications was no.

Even Jesus, the obedient Son, received a no from God. On the night of His betrayal by Judas, He prayed in the garden of Gethsemane, "Abba, Father, . . . everything is possible for you. Take this cup away from me" (Mark 14:36, NIV). But the cup was not removed; Jesus had to endure the passion and the cross. The prayer was not granted, not even to the Son!

You, too, have probably received a no from God; those of us who pray all get them at times. When they come in answer to fervent requests for the healing of a loved one, they seem most difficult to handle. When our prayer is not granted, we feel neglected; we remember those who received a miracle, and we feel slighted; we think that there must be something wrong with our faith, and we feel guilty; we suffer through the hurt of our loss, and we feel deserted. And because we are hurting and feel neglected and slighted and guilty and deserted, we become angry. Questions well up in our minds. Even if we do not voice them to God or to anyone else, they are there; they are old questions.

Does God really say no, or does the Creator of life just not hear the plea? Even if we grant that our Creator is "out there," is also "down here," and that there is a connection between us, does that Giver of Life really hear us? Or, if we are heard, does God simply turn away and ignore us unless it suits the divine purposes to do otherwise? When the prayer is not granted, has it really been attended to?

If it has, then is the promise really trustworthy? Search the Word of God, and the pledge to grant our petitions is there repeatedly.

And whatever you ask in prayer, you will receive, if you
have faith (Matt. 21:22).

Therefore I tell you, whatever you ask in prayer, believe
that you have received it, and it will be yours (Mark 11:24).

Whatever you ask in my name, I will do it that the Father
may be glorified in the Son; if you ask anything in my name,
I will do it (John 14:13-14).

The promises go on (Matt. 7:7-8; Mark 11:23; John 15:7;
16:24). In light of these affirmations, if we are heard and the
answer is no, are we being misled? Is God a liar?

If we cannot believe that God would lie to us, are we
deficient? Is my lack of faith the root of the denied prayer?
Is my belief not strong enough to warrant the granting of my
plea? Is a power absent from my life that ought to be there—
and, if there, would have activated a different response from
God? Did my lack of faith doom my loved one?

These questions can intrude at the time of loss. But, remember, the sin lies not in the questioning; the wrong grows
out of not staying around to hear the answers. So at this
point, we turn to a brief exploration of what prayer is and
how the gift is intended to be used. This will not be a compre-
hensive consideration, for such could not be accomplished in
a book of this nature. I hope it will suffice to provide ade-
quate understandings to the questions we are considering. A
fuller discussion can be found in a work written by O. Hallesby titled simply *Prayer*.[1] Mr. Hallesby's teaching has in-
fluenced my understandings and will be reflected in what is
presented.

Why do we pray? What is the purpose of talking with the
Sovereign of the universe? What is the communication sup-
posed to accomplish? When and how should we engage in
these conversations? People have different understandings

about these things, so there are a variety of responses that come in answer to the questions.

Some believe that prayer is primarily an avenue for making known to God what we need. The prayers of such folk are a string of requests raised in conversations that take place at the time a heartfelt need or desire is being experienced. The scriptural justification cited for this conception is the fact that we are invited by our Lord to bring our petitions— "Ask and it will be given . . ." (Matt. 7:7). But if God is an all-knowing Creator, how can that omniscient Being be unknowledgeable concerning our requirements and desires?

The fact is that God is fully acquainted with all that we need and want. If asking or making known were the only basis for prayer, or the primary purpose of it, praying would be superfluous. In fact, the teaching of Scripture is that such a conception of prayer is a pagan view. The Gospel tells us, "In praying. . . . Do not be like them [the heathen] who heap up empty phrases, for your Father knows what you need before you ask him" (Matt. 6:7-8).

Well, if God knows all our needs and wants, another view of prayer is that it is an entreaty to bring about a change of heart in the Almighty. Prayer in this view is to get God to give us something, to change God's inclinations toward us. But what are these divine inclinations even before our prayers are raised?

The whole testimony of men and women in their experience with the divine, and recorded in Scripture through human history, is that God is good. Jesus made the point in His response to the ruler who addressed Him as "Good Teacher" saying, "Why do you call me good? No one is good but God alone" (Luke 18:19). It is the nature of Goodness

to love; in fact, the nature of Goodness becomes the very
definition of love: "God is love" (1 John 4:8).

The desire of love is to give; that is our understanding of
loving behavior. God's inclination, by nature, is to want to
provide us with all that we need for a full, healthy, and
wholesome life. "Every good endowment and every perfect
gift is from above, coming down from the Father of lights"
(Jas. 1:17). God wants to give us what is good for us and to
keep from us that which will be harmful. If the purpose of
prayer is simply to get God to change His inclinations toward us and give us something, then, again, prayer is superfluous—God already wants to do that!

So if we are invited to ask in prayer, but asking is not the
basic purpose of our praying; and if our prayers are not
necessary to incline God to want to give us things, we are
back to our original question: What is the purpose of prayer?

If, as demonstrated in Chapter 4, people were made for
loving relationship with their Creator, then "man's chief end
is to glorify God" as the opening of the Shorter Catechism
declares. Out of love what else do we have to give the the One
who is the Giver and Sustainer of our lives? This purpose of
life was made clear when Jesus said, "Whatever you ask in
my name, I will do it, that the Father may be glorified in the
Son" (John 14:13). Every act in the creation, even the granting of our prayer requests, is to be directed to glorifying God.
Does it not follow, then, that the gift of prayer was given to
us as a means to support the purpose of human existence, the
glorification of God through loving relationship? But how
would that work?

Prayer is the gift of a channel for communication with that
Power who authored our life. Through that vehicle we render our love in response to what we have received and we

declare the exaltedness that ordained all of which we are a part. We accomplish both of these ends by acknowledging our own helplessness and coming in need to God.

All prayer should center about the fact that we could not exist outside of our Creator, nor could we continue to exist outside of divine grace. Prayer opens our being to God, admitting the divine Power into our distress, our needs, our wants, our confessed helplessness, our life. God knows our situation exactly; God simply wants our invitation to come in to it and help. "For thus says the high and lofty One who inhabits eternity, whose name is Holy: 'I dwell in the high and holy place, and also with him who is of a contrite and humble spirit'" (Isa. 57:15). That invitation to come in, extended in humility and contrition, is a glorification of our Creator.

Our faith that brings us to prayer in the sure knowledge that God is with us, loves us, and will hear and answer our petitions also glorifies God. Faith is our confession that we are the creatures and not God. Without it there can be no prayer, for prayer is our cry of helplessness to the Being we acknowledge as the only One who can rescue us. We surrender our self-centeredness and self-sufficiency when we confess that God is the center of and the power in all of life. That is all our Creator wants from us, that acknowledgment and the opportunity to be a part of our lives. Our faith glorifies God.

Prayer, then, is that condition of heart and mind which brings us to God admitting our helplessness but also declaring with the full knowledge of faith that our cry will be heard and answered. Prayer is that which opens our being to our Creator. "Behold, I stand at the door and knock; if any one hears my voice and opens the door, I will come in to him"

(Rev. 3:20). There is no higher glorification we can render than opening the door to our life.

With this understanding, we are able to see that prayer can be, and so often is, misused. Often we attempt to bend prayer to serve our own gratifications and selfish desires. Prayer then becomes not a vehicle for the glorification of God, but a means for serving our own ends. We come to God only when we want something; we indicate what we desire; we lay out exactly what form the answer should take; and we accuse God if the order is not promptly filled. We do not want God; we want what God can do for us. Those who pray in this fashion attempt to use God and are often angry when they cannot. Among those who see prayer this way, some will turn completely from it and others will use it very infrequently.

If we are honest about it, when we cry over the loss of loved ones are we not crying for ourselves as well as for them? Of course, we feel badly about their suffering and the ending of their lives; such feelings are deep and sincere. We truly wish they could have continued their lives here for their sake. But we wish the same for our sake also. We do not want to suffer the separation, we do not want to endure the loss, and we do not want to experience the pain. In the loss of someone we love, we lose a part of ourselves; we are hurt. We mourn the separation, and we cry over our loss. And, in such circumstances, we may try to use prayer illegitimately.

We may try to bargain, we may seek to influence God's thinking in our favor, we may implore divine Grace for a miracle—none of which serve to glorify God. Then we might say, "Well then, Lord, heal my beloved so that your name will be glorified by the healing." Now that would seem to fulfill the requirements for prayer until we recognize that this is but a form of bargaining. God is worthy to be glorified aside from the gift of any miracle. If we use prayer illegitimately, it cannot work, for then it is not prayer.

Then how shall we pray for the healing of a dying loved one to our Lord who says to us, "Ask, and it will be given you; seek, and you will find; knock, and it will be opened to you. For every one who asks receives, and he who seeks finds, and to him who knocks it will be opened" (Matt. 7:7-8)? Should not our prayer simply confess our helplessness and express our faith that we will be heard, that God already knows our distress, and that in His love the Lord will send an answer that will work for our good? We can ask that life be spared, that healing be granted, that loss be averted, if along with the request we pray "that your name be glorified." If that prayer is sincere, it must include the understanding that healing or the avoidance of loss may not be granted if that would most work to God's glorification. True prayer does not dictate to God, but opens our being to the Lord of heaven and earth, allowing the divine will to work in us.

Now suggesting that our loved one's death can glorify God may be offensive to us and to our conception of a loving Deity. But in our natural self-centeredness, is it not true that, when God does not put the divine Self at our disposal by giving us the answer to prayer that we want, we are offended? Yet whose creation is this? Who knows its origin, purpose, and destiny? Who is best able to determine its (and ours because we are a part of it) ultimate good? Remember the response that came to a questioning Job?

"Who is this that darkens my counsel
   with words without knowledge?
Brace yourself like a man:

I will question you,
and you shall answer me.
"Where were you when I laid the earth's foundation?
Tell me, if you understand.
Who marked off its dimensions? Surely you know!
Who stretched a measuring line across it?
On what were its footings set,
or who laid its cornerstone—
while the morning stars sang together
and all the angels shouted for joy?" (Job 38:2-7, NIV).

When we insist that we be the determiners of what is right and good for us and those we love, we reverse the role of Creator and creature. And isn't that what we so often try to do?

If we find this reality of prayer frustrating, we must examine the genuineness of our faith, of our trust in our Creator. If we want another answer by which we can approach God with a guarantee that our prayer "will work" in terms of our personal, immediate satisfaction, there is none. Either we recognize the supremacy of God, the goodness of God, the love that God has for us, God's ultimate desire to bring us all to that happy destiny we've been promised, and our own helpless situation or we must turn away and face life alone. Since there isn't much that you and I can really control, going through life on our own would seem to be a rather undesirable choice!

Our alternative is to accept the gift of faith that God sends, by which we open our lives to our Lord. In that state of trust we are assured that our prayers are heard and we can say as did Jesus when he prayed before the tomb of his friend Lazarus, "Father, I thank you that you have heard me. I knew that you always hear me" (John 11:41-42, NIV). That answers the first of the three questions initially raised in this chapter. If our loved one dies, if our divorce is not mended, if our job is still lost, even after we have prayed for the miracle, it is not that we have not been heard; it is that the answer has been no.

Can we then trust the promise? That was the second question. The answer is, of course! We must simply understand what the promise is. "Whatever you ask in prayer, you will receive, if you have faith" (Matt. 21:22). As already discussed, that faith is in the supremacy of God, the goodness of God, the love of God for us, and God's desire to work for our good. Therefore, God will not grant requests that will not work for the ultimate good of all.

The answer no comes to some prayers because we do not understand what is in our best interest. "You ask and do not receive, because you ask wrongly, to spend it on your passions" (Jas. 4:3). Could it not be in the best interest of our loved ones to be taken into heaven, freed of the hurts, suffering, and grief of this life to enjoy that realm where "he will dwell with them and they shall be his people, and God himself will be with them; he will wipe away every tear from their eyes, and death shall be no more, neither shall there be mourning nor crying nor pain any more, for the former things have passed away" (Rev. 21:3-4)? Our Lord does not lie; God sees the ultimate good that is beyond our human vision. Whether the answer is a quick and desired yes, or a quiet but definite no, God always has our best interest at heart.

So, now we arrive at the third and final question: Can our lack of faith be the cause of a no answer and, thus, the reason our loved one died? Not if we believe what has been reviewed in this chapter concerning prayer. God does not need our faith as an addendum to divine power in order to act. Asking is not the basic purpose of prayer, and our prayers are not necessary to incline God to want to do things for us—God already wants to do that. God wants and requires our prayer as an admittance to our distress so we can receive divine help. To be true prayer, it must come as a recognition of our helplessness and a belief that our help lies only in our Lord— all of which works to the glory of God. Our lack of faith can only keep God from entering our own distress and working in our life for our good; it does not hamper the good that God wants to do and will do for those about us.

Even in the ungranted request, then, we can see that God is with us, in us, faithfully serving our ultimate interests, which lie beyond our own purview. All we need to do is open the door to our distress through the prayer of faith that humbly acknowledges our own helplessness. When we open the door we have the promise, "I will come in."

If all this is so and the desire of God is always for our best interest, then why is loss such a blow to us; why does it have to hurt so? This is the subject that we will address next.

6
Why Does It Have to Hurt?

People attach themselves to things, all kinds of things—keepsakes, pets, causes, material possessions, occupations, and other people. We all have special gifts or heirlooms which we cherish. Pets often become like one of the family and are sometime treated like children. Gardening, model railroading, boating, and other hobbies can develop into the fabric of our lives so that we literally "love" the activity. Some people do the same with their causes. And so it goes with other things. Parents, children, spouses, other close relatives and intimate friends are categories of people with whom we form bonding relationships.

In the case of loving attachments, the object involved literally becomes incorporated in ourselves, a part of our own self-system. Separation which comes with the loss of any one of these "love" objects brings real emotional trauma. When we lose a keepsake our expression is, "I'm sick about it." If something happens so that we can no longer take part in an activity that we "love doing," we suffer emotionally as we would over the loss of a treasured possession. When a loved one is removed from such an intimate association through any separation—a serious spat, moving away, a child's marriage and relocation, divorce—we are particularly distressed.

Loss through physical death is the ultimate of such emotional suffering.

What follows is based on understanding the process of attachment and the trauma of loss from a faith perspective that accommodates present psychological knowledge. Why is it that in a system established by a loving God we must suffer the physical and emotional pangs of separation? Why does it have to hurt? The answer, as we shall see, is intimately related to the mode in which the creation was made to function. Chapter 4 developed the proposition that people were created for the purpose of being in loving relationship with God and each other through eternity. We must now explore further the implications of that proposition.

The design in which people live out this eternal loving relationship with God has two stages: life on earth and life in heaven. Our life on earth requires no discussion for it is our present reality; it is, therefore, self-evident. But we are promised more than this earthly existence which ends in physical death. "Whoever drinks the water I give him will never thirst. Indeed, the water I give him will become in him a spring of water welling up to eternal life" (John 4:14, NIV). Life in heaven, eternal life, transpires in a relationship with God which becomes face to face. "Now the dwelling of God is with men, and he will live with them" (Rev. 21:3, NIV). Heaven is the name we give to the place where this phase of life occurs. The eternal aspect of our humanity which we call the soul, discussed in Chapter 3, is the part of us that exists in this manner with our Creator. What we experience as physical death is the passage through that valley where ". . . the perishable must clothe itself with the imperishable" (1 Cor. 15:53, NIV). It is the miracle by which we pass from the earthly phase of life into the heavenly phase.

Love is the medium in which both earthly and heavenly life are designed to unfold. Remember the teaching of Jesus when He was asked, "Teacher, which is the great commandment in the law?" He said, "You shall love the Lord your God with all your heart, and with all your soul, and with all your mind." And there was a second which He declared was like the first, "You shall love your neighbor as yourself" (Matt. 22:37-39). What was it that the apostle Paul identified as the most essential ingredient of life? Love! "If I have prophetic powers, and understand all mysteries and all knowledge, and if I have all faith, so as to remove mountains, but have not love, I am nothing" (1 Cor. 13:2). Loving is the fundamental condition of life in the creation because it is basic to wholesome relationships.

Science has made eminently clear that human life is but one of the elements in an immense cosmic system that functions with order and balance. Simple observation tells us that on earth people play a dominant role; you and I and others of our kind are an important controlling factor in what happens here. We design, build, alter, consume, divert, relegate, enhance, destroy, propagate, and otherwise use the ecosystem of which we are a part so that all the other constituents of it were affected.

We also observe that there is a rhythm and relatedness to what we are a part of and that our welfare is caught up in that; people cannot live in disregard of the other parts of the system. If we contaminate the water or pollute the air, we develop illnesses. If we use the wrong propellant in aerosol cans, we can damage the ozone layer which filters the ultraviolet rays from the sun that can be deadly. Acid rain from the combustion of modern industrial plants can kill the flora and fauna necessary to support our own living. Nuclear explo-

sions in the quanities that a thermonuclear war would produce might well bring on a nuclear winter that would have
a devastating affect on all life on earth. We humans now
control the means by which, if we lack regard for the other
elements in our ecosystem, we might literally destroy ourselves.

When we interact reasonably, intelligently, and responsi-
bly—in sum, lovingly—with each other and the other parts
of our system, showing regard for each, then things go better,
civilization moves forward. But when we lose sight of the
unity and oneness of the arrangement, when we elevate self-
desire to the point where it acts greedily and irresponsibly to
satiate our current appetites—in sum, unlovingly—the enterprise does not go well. We hurt each other, we damage our
environment, and we create long-range problems that will
affect our children's children. What God made is meant to
operate in harmonic relationship; love is the basis for such
functioning.

But to love is to become vulnerable; to love is to risk. To
love opens us to the possibility of hurt even if it is applied
with perfection, as we all have learned in the experience of
losing a loved one. But, in addition, hurt can come because
the concept of love has become corrupted. Selfishness and the
brokenness which it has produced in the world has caused
the meaning of loving behavior to become muddled. Because
of the confusion about what love is and how it operates, in
trying to satisfy their desire for it, people follow two general
strategies: the way of *power* and the way of *weakness*. One
becomes a misguided venture which is self-defeating, while
the other turns out to be the only possible route to the
objective.

Some people try to rig life in such a way that they will be

assured their share of what they conceive to be love. Their technique grows out of an inner fear that they will be left alone or that others might not like them or, even worse, may achieve a one-up position over them and use the advantage to hurt them or put them down. People who operate in this fashion strive for power in order to control. They vie for ascendancy and to this end attempt to manipulate others to their own personal advantage. With them, even the expression of loving-like behavior becomes a tool for using people for self-benefit. This kind of relationship diminishes other people by depriving them of their human dignity; it robs them of their humanity by seeking to manipulate them in ways not beneficial to them. In such relationships, no love exists, only an association in which tension is constantly present under the surface. The tension can be created by one person using another or by two individuals trying to use each other.

The other method of seeking to fulfill the need to be loved is through weakness, and it is the only way that the kind of loving designed into creation can be actualized. Weakness is inherent in the fact that loving puts us in a position where we might be hurt. Loving exposes us because it requires a giving of self. Giving self in love is a process of opening ourselves, letting another see and know the inner us, literally bringing them into our self-system. It is the sharing of self for the enhancement of another, but, ultimately, also for our own extension and enrichment. Such sharing and caring is the coming together through which we achieve the fullness of our humanity. We become fully human in our loving relationships with our Creator and each other.

Of course, no one completely bares all to anyone. Psychological health requires that an intimate core of our being remain private. But loving relationship is a mutual openness in which successes and failures are shared, strength and weakness is allowed to show. Its epitome is found in the complete honesty of motive. There is no striving for ascendancy but a readiness to support and encourage. In loving relationships we can experience honest joy in the successes of others because an investment of our own self is a part of the good fortune. We can also sincerely share tears in times of hurt.

To understand the mechanics of this we have to return to the subject of ego boundaries which was opened in Chapter 2. The discussion there was of the process whereby the infant gradually puts into place those boundaries which physically and psychologically mark off each individual. Psychologists call these personal limits "ego boundaries."

In the condition of true loving behavior, we become attracted to an individual (or an object or activity) in whose life we want to make an investment. This investment involves a commitment to nurture something which exists outside of our own self-boundaries. The process of attraction, investment, and commitment to a love object outside ourself is called "cathexis." In this process, we psychologically incorporate a representation of that object into our own self-system. Our loved ones become representively incorporated in ourselves and, thereby, become a part of who we are. We are very literally enhanced and our self-boundaries are extended when we open ourselves to loving relationships.

The use of power to achieve such relationships grows out of fear. The way of weakness in which we literally bring others into our self-identity develops from courage. To open the real self to others is to take a large risk because we have then allowed them past the normal defenses whereby we protect the ego from attack or damage. In that state our honest and open sharing of intimate thoughts and emotions makes us vulnerable. The weaknesses we might show can be used against us. The private longings we confide can be ridiculed. When we expose ourselves to another in this way, we can be used. Worse yet, we can be rejected or suddenly abandoned. In loving, that sensitive inner core which we conceive as "us" can be violated! To love requires the courage to risk!

Then why would we want to open ourselves to the possibility of being hurt through the practice of love? Two factors are involved in our willingness to do that: (1) Our basic nature inclines us in that direction since we were made in the image of God (creatures able to give and receive love); and (2) loving relationship helps us to combat that awful sense of our aloneness.

Vulnerability has been the pattern for relationship in the creation from the very beginning; God took the first risk! The Creator set us free of divine control and allowed human beings the power of choice. Why did God deign to offer these gracious, freewill gifts to those to whom He had no obligation whatsoever to do so? Well it goes part and parcel with being made to love and be loved; this kind of relationship requires freedom. If you and I are to be able to respond to God's love and reflect that in our living in the creation, we need to be free in a way that is different from any of the other living creatures. We have that license, the gift is called free will because we have the liberty to choose between alternatives. We plan, pursue objectives, and decide how to use the materials we have at our disposal. We are also free to pursue or avoid relationships with God or other persons. We can control the nature of those relationships; they can be loving or otherwise.

Love, you see, cannot be ordered. By its very definition, love must come as something freely given. To freely give, one must be under no compulsion to do so. Love must come as an unconstrained act of the individual who gives it. If there is the slightest coercion of any kind, the response elicited could not qualify as loving. In allowing us a free will, God made it possible for us to love; free will is a part of being created in the divine image.

But in doing so God also opened the divine Self to the possibility of hurt. Men and women who were created to glorify God through loving relationship now had the opportunity to use the freedom of choice to turn away from that purpose. The Love that created voluntarily became vulnerable because the design of what was made had to unfold in the context of freedom. The very act of love, by the nature of what it means to open oneself to such a relationship, involves the jeopardy of being hurt.

Did God experience such hurt? Listen to the lament that comes to us through the prophet Isaiah.

> My loved one had a vineyard
>   on a fertile hillside.
> He dug it up and cleared it of stones
>   and planted it with the choicest vines.
> He built a watchtower in it
>   and cut out a winepress as well.
> Then he looked for a crop of good grapes,
>   but it yielded only bad fruit.
>
> What more could have been done for my vineyard
>   than I have done for it?

> When I looked for good grapes,
>   why did it yield only bad? (Isa. 5:1-2,4).

God has felt pain because God has taken the risk of loving that which was created.

God established a creation which is patterned after the divine nature. It is relational; its functional mode is love; it will exist through eternity. For human beings it unfolds in two stages, life on earth and life in heaven; its purpose is the glorification of God through loving relationship in response to God's love. But designed into its very fabric, inherent in the nature of what it means to be human is exposure to the pain of loss. Because we are made for loving relationship, we will at some time hurt.

Such a condition may at first glance appear to be a serious flaw. But what is the alternative? The recourse would be the design of a relational creation that would operate without love. What is the term we use for relationships which are devoid of love? Is it not *selfishness?* Can we not define the unloving condition as the self-centered exploitation of our neighbor and our environment—and, indeed, our God—for the sake of our own immediate appetites? And is it not such a condition that prevails now in our world where love is not the mode of existence? The hurt and injustice involved in the alternative would far exceed that of the present design!

Then why does the Almighty not use His divine power to assure the operation of love, for certainly our world in general is not functioning according to His design? In answering that question, we must take account of our previous discussion: Love cannot be ordered even by a Creator who has all power because love, by its nature, must be freely given. This is the reality which underlies the teaching of Jesus: "For whoever would save his life will lose it" (Matt. 16:25). To find the fullness of wholesome existence in the creation, loving relationship with God and each other, we must give ourselves away (lose ourselves) in the association. But in the giving away, we are enhanced as our own self-boundaries are extended. In loving relationship, we literally become more than we could be by ourselves: "Whoever loses his life for my sake will find it" (Matt. 16:25). When we freely give ourselves in love to God and each other, we find ourselves experiencing the joy and contentment of harmonic relationship, which is the design mode of creation.

But at the death of a loved one, we are plunged into grief and in an instant the joy and contentment seem to be wiped away. Is this two-stage system in which eternal life unfolds another design flaw, for it builds in the hurt of separation? If we love, we will all feel the pain of losing those whom we love when physical death comes.

Again, what might be judged a flaw is part of the design mode. Life is given for the glorification of the Creator through loving relationship in response to divine love. Since love must be freely given, and requires that the power of free choice be granted, the system must provide an opportunity for the exercise of that free choice. Life on earth is that phase of eternal existence in which people are given an opportunity to align themselves with the purpose of creation or turn away from that. The perfect operation of both stages is seen in the life of Jesus of Nazareth. "Let us fix our eyes on Jesus, the author and perfecter of our faith, who for the joy set before him endured the cross, scorning its shame, and sat down at the right hand of the throne of God" (Heb. 12:2, NIV).

In stage 1 we enjoy the opportunity to choose alliance with God which leads to stage 2, eternal existence in heaven. This is the promised hope reflected by the apostle Paul when he wrote,

> I am already being poured out like a drink offering, and the time has come for my departure. I have fought the good fight, I have finished the race, I have kept the faith. Now there is in store for me the crown of righteousness, which the Lord, the righteous Judge, will award me on that day—and not only to me, but also to all who have longed for his appearing (2 Tim. 4:6-8, NIV).

The pain of separation that is built into this two-stage arrangement does not go unattended. The Creator provided in our humanity a capacity to heal. Although there is a wound which exists forever as a hole in our life left by our loved one, there is also a grace which enables us to reconstruct ourselves around that which is not now present and pursue all the other opportunities that remain a part of our future. Life is tenacious; it hangs on, struggles to continue and to grow. This proclivity to rebuild the self in light of the loss is known as the work of grief.

The second consideration which is built into the system to attend the pain of our grief is the promise that we will be united again with those we have lost—the separation is temporary! ". . . and where I am, there shall my servant be also" (John 12:26). This reality was beautifully expressed by Robert Louis Stevenson:

> He is not dead, this friend—not dead
> But, in the path we mortals tread
> Gone some few, trifling steps ahead,
> And nearer to the end;

> So that you too, once past the bend
>   Shall meet again, as face to face,
> this friend you fancy dead.

Our solace comes from the knowledge that our loved one has made the miraculous transition to that place which is free of hurt, suffering, grief, and tears; and that we will one day meet there. In that solace, healing can take place.

It would appear that we have come to a final objection: Why can't an all-powerful God take the hurting out of the love process? Such a removal would change the very character of what love is. Love is the submissive offer of self in commitment to another. What do we offer if not our willingness to open our life, let the "other" come in, and become vulnerable? In our love for God, we make ourselves vulnerable to the unfathomed mystery of life in light of God's proffered love to us. In our love for each other, we expose ourself to the hurt of loss which we know will come as part of the miracle of death. The hurt is the cost of the gift. When we give something that has no cost, we have given nothing! But at the same time is not the hurt also the proof of the love? The hurt is the preciousness that authenticates the value of what we give. The hurt will pass, but the love endures. Life grows out of vulnerability, and this is the mystery of love!

Our story is not yet finished, for God does not leave us at the mercies of our own struggles. Grace operates to impel us toward healing and wholeness; there is a power that is a part of what we are that works to draw us toward our own fulfillment, toward life. It is no accident that life is tenacious, that it struggles to hang on, survive, heal, move forward. In our grief and doubts, that power is operating to ward off the enticements of an evil that would try to capture our soul in a time of weakness. In the next chapter we will try to understand the battle between the force of good and the force of evil that takes place in the life of each one of us.

7
What Are You Doing to Help Us?

When NASA is preparing to launch a vehicle into space, there is a limited period of time when the astrophysical conditions are just right, and to achieve the desired orbit the space vehicle must be launched in that "window." Moments in people's lives, such as the birth of a baby or moving into a new home, are times when we are particularly open to certain sales approaches; entrepreneurs with appropriate goods and services watch for and move in at these times. Other "windows of opportunity" exist in life. The experience of loss is a time when doubts about faith can arise, even when that faith appeared to be firmly rooted, as was the case with the mother of my sister's friend discussed in Chapter 1. There is a force of entropy in life, a power that works against survival, healing, growth, and health for which the time of loss provides a "window" for its nefarious work. It protrudes itself into the hurt, anger, and doubt of loss in an attempt to exploit us for its destructive purposes. It is ready at any time to seize an opportunity to do its work, but the time of loss is one of its particular "windows."

If God is not only "out there" but also "down here" *with* us and even *in* us, how does that presence become an effective power in the time of such an assault on our well-being? We

have explored what we know about the mind and have presented a prima facie case for the unconscious being an avenue
through which our Creator can be a part of what we are. But
what is the reality of that connection in our day-to-day living
when the onslaughts of evil tempt us in our discouragement,
bewilderment, and suffering to abandon the relationship that
God seeks to have with us? Are we on our own? Or is our
Creator a working force in our daily existence who makes a
difference in the outcome of our struggles, if we are open to
that Force and follow His leads? If there is a real connection
between us, what is God doing on a continuing basis to bring
us through these assaults that would turn us to a self-
destructive life-style and help us survive in loving relationship? The answer to these questions will evolve out of an
understanding of the war that takes place within the life of
each one of us.

The force of entropy that works against our growth in life,
which we will call evil, will attempt to turn our honest doubt
into unbelief. Doubt and unbelief are not at all the same
thing. There is nothing wrong in questioning God if we stay
around so God can address our uncertainties—which God
will do even when they are raised in anger. Unbelief, however, keeps a person from having a connection with the
source of life and the end of unbelief is eternal death.

Unbelief, which is a rejection of God's reality, is an attitude of mind which we adopt; it is not forced upon us. It is
an adamant refusal to believe that there is any higher power
in the universe than our own human reason, capabilities, and
motives. It is an arrogant assumption of "godhood" in which
the individual claims the right to establish the purpose of life
and the manner in which this shall be lived out. In the stance
of unbelief, we refuse to see our own smallness, our own

need, our own helplessness, our own errantry. It is an abandonment of rationality which ancient people recognized as the height of foolishness: "The fool says in his heart, 'There is no God' " (Ps. 14:1). Unbelief detaches us from harmonic relationship with the creation, and we are then alienated from God and each other. Its ultimate end is destruction, "For the wages of sin [alienation from God] is death, but the free gift of God is eternal life through Jesus Christ our Lord" (Rom. 6:23).

On the other hand, doubt is not an attribute of our will; it is rather a weakness which comes over us. Hallesby described it as "faith-distress," "faith-suffering," "faith-tribulation." Doubt is an anguish of the most inner part of the self in which our rationality gropes for meaning. Therefore, it is a time of reexamination of belief in search for assurance. If done in the presence of God with an openness to receive, the suffering will end and a new strength will emerge out of the weakness. "Ask and it will be given you; seek, and you will find; knock and it will be opened to you. For every one who asks receives, and he who seeks finds, and to him who knocks it will be opened" (Matt. 7:7-8). But the force of evil that entices us toward destruction, rather than health and wholeness, will attempt to move us through doubt into unbelief. It is necessary then to understand the reality of evil's intrusion into our life and the countering force of Grace which always acts in opposition to that invasion.

It is not uncommon to experience the sensation of having two natures or two wills within us. The feeling is manifest in the resolutions we make but fail to keep, the hurts we inflict and then regret, and the aspirations we conceive but to which we never quite rise. The apostle Paul described the condition in his own life when he wrote to the Romans, "I know that nothing good lives in me, that is, in my sinful nature. For I have the desire to do what is good, but I cannot carry it out. For what I do is not the good I want to do; no, the evil I do not want to do—this I keep on doing" (7:18-19, NIV). This double-mindedness is analogous to the effect of two forces which impinge upon our lives, each seeking to propel us in an opposite direction. One force urges us to grow, to develop, to become better; the other works to block our growth and push us in the direction of disintegration. These forces emanate from Goodness and evil.

Carl Jung, the noted psychiatrist, observed on the basis of his study and experience that "everything living strives for wholeness."[1] That means that there is a natural bent in all of us to struggle to become more than we presently are, that is to move toward fulfillment—and it is something which is observable. Eric Berne, a psychiatrist known as the father of transactional analysis, made the following observation regarding the phenomenon: "But there is something beyond all this—some force which derives people to grow, progress, and do better. . . . Psychiatrists and psychologists know little or nothing about this . . . part. Religious people might say it was the soul."[2] Scott Peck, who also is a physician, sees this empowerment operating in the realm of physical health as well as mental wholeness. After building a basis for the statement, he wrote, "We can therefore say the same thing about physical disorders that we said about mental disorders: There is a force, the mechanisms of which we do not fully understand, that seems to operate routinely in most people to protect and encourage their physical health even under the most adverse conditions."[3] This force motivates us toward mature love, sharing, and joyful, cooperative up-building. Its effect is like a built-in *life wish* because it spurs us toward healing and positive growth.

The power behind this force is the substance of the gift of life; it is the wellspring of our aliveness; it is the source of energy that empowers our being. Without it there is no life. By definition it comes from the Creator of Life. "Then the Lord God formed man of dust from the ground, and breathed into his nostrils the breath of life; and man became a living being" (Gen. 2:7). We should not be distressed that we cannot find it in our bodies because, in this regard, we are no more or less knowledgeable than we are concerning the basics of other phenomena associated with our existence.

I am indebted to Scott Peck for the insight concerning our ignorance when it comes to understanding root causes. Peck points out that we can trace particular illnesses to a specific bacteria or virus. But the question we cannot answer concerning the cause of a malady is why the organism, which may be present in 85 percent of the cultures taken from a general population, produces sickness in only a few. Similarly, we know that it is the force of gravity that keeps the heavenly bodies in their respective relationships. What we do not know is the seat of the power which makes the equation $F = G (M_1M_2/d^2)$ a true statement concerning the mutual attraction that exists between particles of matter. Scientists can only say that the forces controlling the motion of the planets are due to a single unknown cause. So it is then that we are aware of our aliveness, we observe the effects of an energy that empowers our existence and pushes us toward growth, but we cannot further locate its source except as it has been made known through divine self-revelation to be our Creator God.

But we recognize another power operating upon us, which

works to counteract our healing, growth, and development, and drives us toward self-destruction. It powers a side of ourselves that we would rather not look at, an aspect we would prefer to deny, but a part of our self that is there and must be acknowledged. Jung saw it in us and referred to it as our "shadow side." It is that bent within each of us that activates hostility, unreasoned anger, cruelty, and self-injury. Its effect is like a built-in *death wish,* for it is a self-destructive mechanism.

From where does the power of evil come? Various answers have been given. We shall examine two of the more prominent and then proceed to a conclusion that may give us the only valid answer we can achieve.

Some have attributed the generation of an evil force to God. It was created, this reasoning goes, as an alternative, a choice so that humanity's free will could be operative. If there is no choice, the argument says, there is no real freedom to choose. Therefore, claim the proponents of this view, the One who bestowed the power of life and growth also generated the force which urges us toward death and destruction.

But the theory fails on a very basic point. What God made, He verified as "good." Good in this context has the meaning that what was made was created in conformity with the purpose of creation: loving relationship through eternity. Evil is in mortal combat with this purpose; it seeks to promote conflict and annihilation. Since evil is at odds with creation's goal, this force could not have been generated by the same Creator who saw ". . . everything that he had made, and behold, it was very good" (Gen. 1:31). "If a kingdom is divided against itself, that kingdom cannot stand" (Mark 3:24, NIV). The theory is not credible, neither logically nor theologically.

But the failure of the theory which would make God responsible for the force of evil has led others to claim that there must then be two cosmic powers—a good God that wears the white hat, so to speak, and a bad god who robes in black. This reasoning postulates two deities pitted against each other in mortal combat for the cosmos. It defines a universe which has a dual nature: the evil world made by a lower creator-god in which we now live and the heavenly kingdom made by the God of mercy revealed in Jesus Christ. The view goes back to early Christianity, but it is a concept which the church has consistently opposed and rejected with good reason.

The theory has been repudiated by Christians because it attempts to explain evil and the universe with a purely human concept which is based on reasoning that is hard to understand; it does not conform to logic or Scripture. Speaking logically, there can be only one source for our being. Life and the reality of which it is a part can only have one origin; there cannot (logically "cannot") be two "ultimate" causes. There can only be one First Cause. Thus, logic mitigates against the proposition.

But further, this dualistic model would destroy the Creator's sovereignty. It proposes a reality which goes counter to scriptural teaching because it divides and erodes God's omnipotence. Such a position ignores the evidence of all Scripture which supports the validity of Israel's creedal affirmation: "Hear O Israel; the Lord our God is one Lord" (Deut. 6:4). It violates the testimony of God incarnate in Jesus Christ which addresses God as "Lord of heaven and earth" (Matt. 11:25).

The fact of the matter is that the human mind is not capable of conceiving a completely definitive and integrated formulation of the entire universe. Human intelligence cannot circumscribe God and His creation. God's mind and its conceptions exceed our rational capacities. All we are capable of knowing is what our intelligence can discover or deduce through our contacts with the parts of God's system that we live in and what the self-revelation which our Creator chooses to open to us reveals. We do not have all the pieces; therefore, we cannot complete the puzzle on our own.

The rejection of both of these theories relative to the origin of evil leaves us with an unresolved tension: How can evil successfully exist in the world as an opponent to the Creator who is the one, all-powerful, exclusive God of the universe who is in mortal opposition to evil? Such a tension creates an anxiety in us since we cannot solve its dilemma. But as we just noted above, a completely definitive formulation of the entire universe is beyond our rational processes, and what is not yet revealed we must live with as a mystery.

With this we come to the crux of our search: There is a mystery about evil that must leave us without a simple answer concerning its origination. But our lack of understanding is no more than the case with so many other facets of our knowledge. What we have come to see is that the more we learn, the more we discover how much we still do not know. New knowledge leads us to more precise conceptions of reality, but these in turn open further questions.

Scott Peck discussed this in relation to the uncomfortableness we experience over not being able to grasp the totality of evil and come up with a definitive explanation that illuminates all of its mystery. Peck explained, "The understanding of basic reality is never something we achieve; it is only something that can be approached. And, in fact, the closer we approach it the more we realize we do not understand—

the more we stand in awe of its mystery."[4] We must accept the origin of evil as such an awesome mystery just as we must do concerning the origin of God who has given us life and the power to become.

To get back to our original thought, our lives are the site of a battle between the force of life that impels us toward the attainment of our fullest human potentiality and the force of evil that entices us to a denial of what we were created to be and, as a consequence, self-destruction.

But there is a third factor in the equation which defines this contest, and it has a significant effect on the tilt of the balance; *we* are also a force to be reckoned with in the determination of outcomes. Our free will, which is a mark of our humanity, is the source of that power. The gift of life included a freedom to choose and that means both good and evil require our participation in their causes. We can choose to participate in our own growth and development to achieve the fullness of our humanity, or we can yield to the enticements which lead to conflict and destruction.

The reality of all this is that as a person we are involved in our own development and healing (healing is an aspect of growth: the ability to repair injury and go on). Cooperation with that power of grace that motivates us to push forward, pick ourselves up when hurt, seek healing, and continue toward the fullest development of our humanity leads to that wholeness which Israel calls *shalom*. The journey toward completion of our human potential is what we term *spiritual growth.*

Spiritual growth is the conscious progress of an individual toward a loving relationship with God and others. It is the submission of our free will to God in response to the Creator's free gift of life and freedom. It is our willingness to risk the requirements that will develop from that surrender and to do the work involved in the attainment of the purpose of creation. It is our readiness to make the effort and to apply the discipline which are always involved in any kind of growth.

The journey down such a path has been beautifully and insightfully discussed by Scott Peck in his book *The Road Less Traveled.* The point of it all is to achieve our human potential, the fulfillment of what we are designed to be. As Dr. Peck explained, "We are born that we might become, as conscious individuals, a new life form of God."[5] Scripture conveys the same thought, saying, "He has given us his promises, great beyond all price, and through them you may escape the corruption with which lust has infected the world, and come to share in the very being of God" (2 Pet. 1:4, NEB).

The intent of evil is to prevent spiritual growth and thwart our maturing into this new life form. The problem in our unloving world is that people have yielded to the tempting, prideful desire to compete with God and become gods on their own. We want to set the purpose of life (which is always self-centered when we do it) and decide the mode in which that purpose is to unfold (which in selfishness is always "unloving"). Long eons ago people bought into evil's great lie which said if we disobey God, "You will not surely die. For God knows that when you eat of it [the forbidden fruit] your eyes will be opened, and you will be like God, knowing good and evil" (Gen. 3:4-5, NIV). When we bought into that false doctrine, humanity's perception of what life was to be was distorted.

Conversion is the reorientation of our perspective from the false pretense of the "great lie" to the "truth" of loving fellowship. *To convert* means "to turn." *Conversion,* then, is the changing of position from a self-centered way of viewing life to one in which loving relationship with God and others becomes central. It is a rejection of the lie and an acceptance of God's truth regarding the purpose of the creation. Ever since human beings used their freedom to turn away from relationship with their Creator and pursue the purposes of their own vanity, God's message has been that they should return. "Repent and turn from all your transgressions, lest iniquity be your ruin" (Ezek. 18:30). The message of Jesus of Nazareth in his ministry was "Repent for the kingdom of heaven is at hand" (Matt. 4:17). The parable of the prodigal son (Luke 15:11-24) is the most succinct and poignant statement of the offer that has been made to humanity to return to the intended relationship with God.

As Henri Nouwen put it, "Conversion is the discovery of the possibility of love."[6] It occurs when we are brought to realize that evil has enticed us into a life of strife and conflict. It is the discovery of grace, God's forgiveness, and empowerment to heal and grow. It is that "more excellent" way of which Paul wrote:

> Love is patient and kind; love is not jealous or boastful; it is not arrogant or rude. Love does not insist on its own way; it is not irritable or resentful; it does not rejoice in wrong, but rejoices in the right. Love bears all things, believes all things, . . . endures all things. Love never ends" (1 Cor. 13:4-8).

Loving relationship with God and each other, then, is the actualizing condition by which we are led into the eternal existence for which creation is designed. It is the route by which we come to fulfillment as human beings and find that Power within us that promotes our healing at the time of loss. It is the destination of our journey down the road of spiritual growth. The pursuit of this condition is the effort from which evil constantly tries to turn us aside. But we are not alone in the struggle against evil's efforts since grace is a constant force in our daily existence; God is with us and in us, seeking always to promote healing and wholeness. The catch is that we must align ourselves with that life-building Power; we must be participants in our own development. The next chapter will unfold some observations about that.

8
What Can We Do to Help Ourselves?

If we are willing to open ourselves to love, it will touch us and transform us mysteriously through a process that we can perceive but cannot fully explain. That happened to Jack Murphy of Orlando, Florida. Jack's life contained an emptiness which he seemed unable to fill. He wrote:

> As a young man I had no trouble being successful, whether it was in a tree trimming business, a lawn and pool maintence service, or a nursery. But after the successes I'd wonder, "Is this it? Is this what I'm going to do the rest of my life?" There was an emptiness . . . a void.[1]

In an effort to fill that void "Murph the Surf," as he became known, pursued a life that included abuse of alcohol and narcotics, partying, and fast cars. He developed an attitude that was cynical and sarcastic, coming to a point where he just didn't care. In his bitterness he said, "I'll make my own rules. It seems like money is the answer, so I'll get a lot of money."[2]

In the pursuit of wealth, Jack Murphy became a jewel thief and was as successful at this as he had been in his business ventures. His notoriety as a thief came first with the theft of the Star of India sapphire and several other famous gems

from the American Museum of Natural History in New
York City. He was talented in what he did and daring in his
doing it. But, at the age of twenty-nine, the long arm of the
justice system snared him. He was sentenced to two life terms
plus twenty years in the Florida State Prison.

In prison Jack devised a plan to maintain his physical,
intellectual, social, and emotional health; despite all that he
did the big void was still there. The first evidence that something outside himself was available to make a difference in
his life came in the words of a prison chaplain. The chaplain
told Jack, "Jesus loves you. God almighty loves you. God,
the creator, has a plan for you and you can know him in a
personal relationship through his Son Jesus, who died for
your sins."[3] Jack Murphy could not understand that message
at that time, and he chased the chaplain away.

But that message was seen with a new perspective when
someone told Jack, "Murph, you need a manager." Jack
Murphy knew that his life wasn't working and that he
needed help. Jesus as a manager who could direct and guide
him made some sense. With this new perspective, Jack asked
the Lord into his life. From that time Jack Murphy's life was
literally turned around. He began to live in a different way,
with a different perspective. In some mysterious way, fifteen
years were suddenly removed from his parole date and in
1984 the gates of the prison were opened. Jack Murphy was
again a free man and, for the first time in his life, free of the
void that had plagued him. He now has his own prison
ministry in which he witnesses to God's love. Concerning
what happened to him, Jack Murphy said, "God lifted me
and I experienced that peace that passes all understanding
that Paul spoke about. . . . I thought I was losing it because
you should not feel that good in prison. But the peace of God

was working when I gave it all to him."[4] That's the way that God's love is; if we open ourselves to it we find it has somehow already touched us and holds us in its grasp.

· But how do we open ourselves to a Power that in our moment of loss can seem so distant and so quiet in light of the no we received in answer to our plea? In the chapters of this book we have traced the realities of that quietness and that distance through the questions that pop into our consciousness and are there even if we never voice them aloud. Loss is a time of barrenness for us. It is a time of aloneness. It is as if a deep darkness is upon us such as that expressed in Michel Quoist's prayer, "It Is Dark."

> Lord, it is dark.
> Lord, are you here in my darkness?
>
> ....
> I am alone.
> You have taken me far, Lord; trusting I followed you,
>   and you walked by side,
> And now, in the middle of the desert, at night,
>   suddenly you have disappeared.
> I call, and you do not answer.
> I search, and I do not find you.
> I have left everything, and now I am left alone.
> Your absence is my suffering.
>
> Lord, it is dark.
> Lord, are you here in my darkness?[5]

How are we to be open at a time when we feel so closed?

God knows our condition and does not forget the covenant made, "Lo, I am with you always" (Matt. 28:20). In our episode of darkness, we may feel alone but that Presence of grace is there. That truth is so poignantly portrayed in that widely circulated piece "Footprints." The passage recounts how a man, in a dream, had flashbacks of his life and for each scene there were two sets of footprints in the sand, his and the Lord's. But he also saw that at the lowest and saddest times of life there were only one set of prints. So he asked the Lord, "I don't understand why when I needed you most you would leave me." The Lord replied, "My precious child, . . . I would never leave you . . . when you see only one set of footprints, it was then that I carried you."

Being open to God in our life involves trust, the sure knowledge that the Lord is there. Our whole loving relationship with our Creator unfolds in the trust that we call faith. This fact is seen in the teaching of the gospel that "unless you change and become like little children, you will never enter the kingdom of heaven" (Matt. 18:3, NIV). The preeminent characteristic of the young child is trust. To little children, parents and adults are like gods—all-powerful and all-knowing. In those adults the young child trusts implicitly. The small child's powerlessness finds its security in the power of the parent to provide. The very young turn in confidence to mother and dad for sustenance, for understanding, for reassurance, for protection, and for comforting. They know that their welfare lies completely in the caring affection of the parent, and they are fully accepting of that condition. This kind of confidence is what the Parent of all life desires from His human creations.

God seeks that relationship with us actively by making the covenant "I am with you always" a functional reality in each life. God is literally with us by being in us, a part of what we are. Even though the Creator desires this trusting relationship and literally can be a functional part of our humanity, we can close ourselves to the overture; we can withhold our trust and refuse to surrender.

Over long eons of time, men and women have chosen to trust in themselves—their own intelligence, their own abilities, their own wisdom, their own conception of what life is all about. In taking that stance we have ignored the spiritual aspects of our humanity because we have felt that these have no bearing on our day-to-day living; we don't want or need God's input, or we want it only on our terms. Because the human race has so neglected its "soul," many of us have lost contact with it.

When men and women became so closed to the Divine presence in their human nature that they would not attend its signals or hear its voice, God acted in what amounted to a new creation: God broke into human history by becoming incarnate in the person of Jesus of Nazareth. The radical nature of this act lies in the fact that God became human, not a lesser god; He "emptied himself [of equality with God] . . . taking the form of a servant" (Phil. 2:7,). The Creator came to demonstrate the way of love, to declare that God's kingdom was a reality and to provide a method for our reconciliation.

But this does not come through to us with crystal clarity: It is revealed as paradox, it operates in mystery, and its understanding requires trust. "For now we see in a mirror dimly" as the apostle Paul put it (1 Cor. 13:12). "An evil and adulterous generation seeks for a sign; but no sign shall be given to it," Jesus said (Matt. 12:39). Why is it that we are not allowed a direct view or given a clear sign? Is the reason, perhaps, that the sign and the direct connection are already present in our very being, in what we are? "The kingdom of God does not come visibly, nor will people say, 'Here it is,' or 'There it is,' because the kingdom of God is within you" (Luke 17:20-21,NIV). The sign is embedded in our humanity.

A basic paradox of Christianity is that God is with us and in us, contrary to the appearance of the opposite. In the incarnation God came among us, but people did not know His presence. Jesus did not appear triumphant in glory as we would expect the Ruler of the universe to do; He came humbly as a servant in the guise of a stranger. He was crucified by the evil to which men and women had been enticed and which had drawn them into its diabolical self so that they acted as evil. Humanity was so caught in evil's power that the human beings who were created in the image of Love no longer recognized Love; they did not accept its self-giving character; they did not tolerate its truth in the face of the great lie they were trying to live. To keep their lie intact, they had to blot out that which exposed it: Love was crucified and buried in a tomb. Religion was perversely made the agency of evil's cause; ironically, it was the priests who instigated the conspiracy (Matt. 26:3-5). The denial of what people were created to be, evident in that act, still goes on.

But at this very point, we come again to the paradox of love: When it is weakest and most vulnerable, Love achieves its greatest strength. "God chose what is weak in the world to shame the strong" (1 Cor. 1:27). Jesus reached out to the despairing to comfort them and to care for them. He lived in poverty to make protest to social and economic injustice. He cried for a people who killed their prophets and stoned those sent to reawaken them to their inborn nature. The Man of peace was taken in violence and offered no defense against those who conspired to falsely accuse. When that person, Jesus, did not run but gave Himself up to crucifixion to make

God's point to a twisted humanity, the evil to which men and women had willfully yielded themselves was exposed; humanity's degradation stood bare before all history. The power of that conviction can be understood in our inability to cover up the disgrace or erase it from our memory. From the depths of two thousand years it continues to confront every age!

Its power is also displayed in the growth of the God's church. Evil killed the physical body of Jesus, but it could not obliterate the Spirit of God. Out of the condition of annihilation, the church came to life; annihilation was the necessary precondition to resurrection. Weakness lead to death, but death was only a backdrop for resurrection. In the event that we know as Pentecost (Acts 2), certain people received the sign that Christ's living Spirit was upon them, empowering them to carry out the Great Commission to "make disciples of all nations" (Matt. 28:19).

Paradox involves mystery, for we cannot explain how contradictory alternatives are at the same time true. But the mystery leads us to ask, Why does our Creator deal with us in this way? Why doesn't God come and stand before us in full view? Why does the Almighty act through weakness when God is all-powerful? Why is it that God is with us, even in us, but is hidden from us so that we can never pinpoint the location? Why is it that God will speak to us, but does so in ways that we do not hear a voice and can deny the communication? If our Creator comes to us, why is it we cannot summon God at will? Why does God pull us toward the divine Self, but in a way that always leaves us open to doubt that influence? Why does God work through paradox and hide in mystery? If God is with us, why does Divinity stand veiled by secrecy? Our's is often the same frustration expressed by the Temple priests when they asked Jesus, "How long will you keep us in suspense? If you are the Christ, tell us plainly" (John 10:24, NIV).

But hiddenness is in the very nature of the One to whom we give the name God. God is the veiled Power who out of a void created us and that of which we are a part; only God can know God. If it were otherwise, God would not be God. When the Almighty chooses to reveal Himself, that revelation serves only to disclose who God is—the Hidden One. The more we come to know our Creator, the more exalted and concealed the divine Person becomes. This knowledge only heightens our appreciation of the gracious condescension of One in seeking relationship with us.

God's hiddenness also has a connection with human rebellion. The divine Presence comes to us in obscure forms and mysterious pathways because, in the association, men and women have sought to be the boss. We have tried to use God for our own ends rather than allowing ourselves to be used in the Creator's purpose for life. God hides because men and women try to force their will upon the One who created us to be in loving subservience to Holy Love.

This willfulness is embedded in our ways, even in the way we come into the Christian fellowship. Many join the church, declare themselves to be God's people, but never really surrender their will in trust. They worship and pray but continue to make the decisions about what they will and will not do on the basis of their own desires. The church and God's mission are not given priority in the daily schedule; these are attended to when they do not interfere with the things that we really want to do. There are reservations connected with our coming to God, for we are not sure we will want to do all that may be asked of us. We draw limits and set boundaries beyond which we will not go, will not give, will not do. We continue to try to set the terms of the relationship!

Even in our prayers we can see the attempt to try to control. When we pray we ask for things that we want and that's all right; we are told we should ask. But if events do not develop in the way we have requested, if our desires are not met in the way we prescribed, we charge God with having left us or, at the least, not having listened to us. Often prayer becomes an attempt to manipulate God to our way of thinking. Rather than a seeking of the divine will for our lives, prayer is often an effort to have God let us have things our way.

We try to assure that no matter what the rules, we will be able to gain the objectives in life that we have established for ourselves. We hear the holy commandment that we should love God and our neighbor, we read the admonition to treat others as we would like them to treat us, but we invent subterfuges whereby we twist the teachings from their intent to our intentions. Our rationalizations are designed to fool even ourselves so that when exposed, as will happen at times with the best of schemes, we cry out in purported innocence.

The result is that we are not ready for direct encounter with God. As we have seen, our free will is a necessary condition to our being able to be loving creatures. During our earthly existence, we have the opportunity to exercise the choices growing out of that gift of freedom. But if our Creator came before us in the full majesty and power of holy glory, our only alternative would be submission; we could not stand before such awesomeness. "You cannot see my face; for man shall not see me and live" (Ex. 33:20). In such circumstances, our freedom of choice would disappear, swept away by the unveiled Immanence; our will could not but be overwhelmed in such a divine confrontation, and our power of choice would disintegrate.

If that were to happen now, our association with God would not develop from loving response to the Creator's love for us; it would grow out of awe and shock. The relationship then would not be a result of our willful choice exercised in freedom; it would not be motivated by love. But revelation tells us that the glorification of God through a loving relationship with God and each other is the purpose of creation. So from the hiddenness of paradox and mystery, God continues to extend the opportunity of eternal, loving fellowship and works to bring the creation to the fullness of its divine purpose. God is with us and in us, urging us to the fulfillment of our destiny and ready to empower that fulfillment, as we obediently open ourselves through trust to the divine reality in life.

Because of this hiddenness, we cannot deal with God simply through our intellect. God avoids being pinned down by empirical proof and can only be approached through the trust that we call faith. Lacking faith "you shall indeed hear but never understand, and you shall indeed see but never perceive" (Matt. 13:14). Loving, as we have seen, entails vulnerability. In faith we are vulnerable to God's promises, but make ourselves so because we trust the purpose of the One who gave us life. In faith we know that Holy Love will not use our devotion or abuse our response. In effect, we make ourselves vulnerable to the mystery of God, and we do it through the humility of trusting obedience to the divine purpose for life.

In the dark hours of our loss and hurt, we can trust the Love that gave us life because it has always been there for us, for all humanity, even though, at times, it may seem distant and quiet. The rationale for such a trust is beautifully stated in the following personal answer to doubt.

> I know this love because I have *experienced* it, historically through a tradition, immediately through a thousand persons, strong and weak, sick and well, paragons and criminals, saints and self-styled unbelievers, family and strangers. I have known it coming into my life and flowing from me (sometimes against contrary feelings) to others. Why? What is it? More and more, I want to say, "Who is he?"—this mysterious spirit that heals, binds us together, gives up lifeboat space, rebuilds broken families, heals the psychotically estranged, evokes tenderness, forgiveness, hope? Who is he that conceived the delicate wonder of childhood, the sensuous warmth of healthy mature beauty, the patinaed, gnarled gray wisdom of age, the endless mystery of life and death? I don't *know,* but I trust his love; I sense his presence; I have felt his power.[6]

As we move into the mystery through faith, we find healing for hurt miraculously comes. Out of the barrenness of our grief, we will find a fuller revelation of grace—the experience is a refining, an edification. It is life transcending itself in a process of becoming. It is a resurrection! If we are patient and remain open in confident trust, it comes as a divine gift. Albert Schweitzer said it most eloquently, "And to those who obey him, whether they be wise or simple, he will reveal himself in the toils, the conflicts, the sufferings which they shall pass through, and, as an ineffable mystery, they shall learn in their own experience who he is."[7]

In such a way does grace lead us to Himself in the experience of loss.

9
Living with God in Loss

In this book I have set down a story about how God can and will deal with us through all the exigencies of profound loss. In the telling I have shared some of my personal story, hoping to touch a strand of experience in each reader's life that we share through our common humanity. We are all hurt by loss. At this point I have finished the account of the reality of God, the operation of divine grace in our lives, and the availability of that grace to all of us if we are open to it. In this final chapter, I wish to share a few concluding observations that I believe we should keep in mind as we endeavor to live with God through our experience of loss. They are observations that will complete the story of my journey through loss.

The ancient psalmist cried my prayer thousands of years before it passed through my lips, "Out of the depths I cry to thee, O Lord! Lord, hear my voice!" (Ps. 130:1). When my younger son died of cancer it was the second such loss that my wife and I had experienced. Four years prior we had lost our older son through a terrible tragedy. There is no question that we were in the depths of despair like none other we had ever experienced. My loss was real, the most profound I could ever experience, and my injured cry was a moan that welled up from the very center of my being. I prayed for the divine help that I needed to sustain me; it came. It came not in a swift momentary event, but gradually as I lived out the succeeding days and months. As I lived through my experience with God, I gained helpful insights about my journey.

First, I am now more convinced than ever that in the event of severe hurt we must look outward from self if we are to be healed. By looking outward I found God to be with me. Dwelling upon our own inner trauma, although it is there and we feel it in very significant ways, works to magnify rather than soothe the injury. Focusing on self causes our wound to become the paramount essence of our daily journey; rather than bringing healing, it promotes continued bleeding.

I am reminded of an incident that was reported concerning one of the Menninger brothers who established the well-known Menninger Clinic. This psychiatrist had just given a talk to a group of lay persons and was entertaining questions from the audience after his presentation. One person asked, "What should one do if he finds himself so stressed-out that he believes that it is possible that he might go into a complete collapse?" Now I am sure that many folk in that crowd thought that this learned physician was going to advise that such a person should certainly seek professional help immediately. But that is not at all what the doctor counseled. Instead, he made a short and simple statement which omitted completely seeking any medical help. Dr. Menninger said, "I would tell such a person to seek out someone who needed help and then become involved in helping them." We must look outward from self if we are to find the healing we need in our own lives.

This understanding is related to what I believe is one of

our very basic problems as people. In our tendency to focus on self, we lose the attachment with God and others that is necessary to the fulfillment of our humanity, our own healthy existence if you will. Each of us is a part of a system that must function in harmonic relationship with all the other parts, as was discussed in Chapter 6. When things and people matter only as means to support or gratify our own personal needs, we have lost a vital perspective. Such a detachment reflects a "lostness" in which there is no relationship with anything higher or more profound than myself and the present moment. In such a position we forget who we are, that is, we lose the meaning of our humanity. A recent comment in a city newspaper makes the point. "Modern man is becoming increasingly lost. He does not understand who he is, why life is as it is, where he is going, or what to do about air pollution, crab grass, noise, lawlessness, and the fact that he can't sleep at night."

Our sleeplessness; our increasing dependence on drugs— both prescribed and illicit; the boredom we try to obliterate by filling life with possessions; the emptiness we fill with the trivia of modern television; the overemphasized concern with sexual gratification; a soaring divorce rate; the abuse which runs rampant in our families; the violence of our society; terrorism in whose clutches civilized decency lies victim; the tensions we cannot solve in Northern Ireland, the Near East, and Central America—and the list could go on—are all symptoms of the dilemma. Humanity is lost, and we cannot find ourselves. By focusing solely on ourselves, we have no memory of where we came from, no perception of our purpose for being here. Through a visage that has turned inward, we have forgotten our identity; we are unable to see who we were created to be.

When we lose sight of who we were created to be and, thus, ignore the unity of that of which we are a part, we are then estranged from it; we live in a state of alienation. Alienation is a condition of attachment to self that brings about a detachment from other persons and other things. In that condition the rest of the world is seen as existing only for personal benefit. Other people, other life, other things—which are designed to function cooperatively for mutual enhancement —are profaned by a self-centered focus that "uses" rather than shares. An extreme example of this estrangement is evidenced in the thinking of Adolf Eichmann, the Nazi war criminal, which is reported from a deposition given to an Israeli police superintendent.

> He deplored what he saw: he found the screams of people strangling in the gas trucks in Poland unbearable; a fountain of blood, which gurgled up through the ground of a mass grave revolted him. Specifically, somewhere near Minsk, he saw naked Jews moving forward to the edge of a pit where the SS riflemen shot them; some shots were sloppy, the half-dead squirmed, so they fired into the heaped bodies as well. Eichmann reported this scene to an SS leader in Lemburg. " 'Yes, that is horrible,' I said to him. 'There the young people are being educated to become sadists. . . . How can you just bang into a pile of people, women and children, how is that possible?' I said, 'this can't be. The people must either turn crazy or become sadists. Our own people.' "[1]

Eichmann gave no thought whatsoever to the people being murdered. He was concerned about the effects these things had on him and on the nerves of his own people, the young men in the SS troops.

To profane is to violate by unworthy use—it debases that which is so used. Eichmann's thinking is an extreme example, but there are other degrees of profanation that strike closer to where most of us live. When we ravage nature to feed our own greed, when we manipulate other people for our own advantage, when we take from our community more than we are willing to contribute to it, when we ignore the plight of the destitute, when we do not cry out against injustice, when we will not see our neighbor's hurt and respond to it, we are alienated.

In that condition of self-centeredness, we cannot heal, either as individuals or as a human race. When we do not function as a part of the larger context, we perpetuate and magnify our woundedness. We must look outward from self if we are to be healed, both as individuals and as a people. We are involved in our own rehabilitation and that involvement is with the purpose for which human life was given: loving relationship with God and each other through eternity.

A second observation I would make about living with God through the experience of loss is that we should look for God in the ordinary rather than the extraordinary. When my prayer for the life of my son did not receive an affirmative response, I had to remember that the everyday events of living are the normal channels through which God will work in our life. Having failed to get the miracle that would have reversed the course of the cancer that was devouring the life of my son, I could have become devastated. In fact, a friend put the question to me, "How do you keep from cursing God?" Rather than curse God, my inclination at that time was to find my Lord somewhere in what was happening to me. I found God miraculously working in the ordinary.

Here I am speaking of the "miraculous" as an act of God and not just in the more common understanding as an extraordinary divine intervention in life. A miracle is an event that transcends our knowledge of the laws of nature. Such events can occur as supernatural marvels that transfix us or as acts that can happen through the normal pulses of life— events that send us in certain directions, bring thoughts into our consciousness, empower us to do or to endure what otherwise we could not find possible. If we look for God only in the gigantic episodes of life, we are very apt to miss the divine Presence, for those miracles are, indeed, few and far between. In such case we will be very susceptible to the erroneous inclination that God has deserted us and is nowhere about. But if we look for our Lord in the day-to-day events of our comings and goings we will find that we are not alone. Jane's story reflects what I am talking about here.

Jane came to see what I call the miracle of the ordinary in the course of her unfolding Christian experience. Jane appeared in the congregation of our church one Sunday morning. I later learned that she had not been near a church for fifteen or more years. She came to worship with us on that particular day because she was looking for a healing that she had not been able to find through traditional psychotherapy.

Jane had suffered the effects of a mental condition known as borderline personality disorder, a condition in which she experienced psychotic episodes. Personality disorders are difficult to treat, but Jane was able to get effective psychiatric help over the course of several years before I knew her. With this professional help, she was freed from the psychotic symptomology and improved to the point where she was able to earn a college degree and certification as a secondary school teacher.

But when she appeared in our church, her problems were far from over; that is why she had come. She knew that she needed help, and she had come seeking God's aid, somehow sensing that human therapy had done all it could for her. Jane began to talk with me on a regular basis about her condition. She was fearful, insecure, suffering a constant depression, and in a marriage that was not going well. Although she had attained certification, she could not bring herself to apply for a teaching position.

As we talked and prayed together over the course of several weeks, Jane came to the point where she was able to send out her applications—and she was hired! She began to teach, continued to worship with us, and became active in the Sunday School. As she was able to turn her perspective outward to her students, her church, and her Sunday School, she was able to function better, more normally, although she still fought bouts of depression.

Jane's continuing frustration with depression caused her to raise this question, "Where is God in all this? I feel like I am doing everything by my own efforts. I pray for relief but I do not see any response. Why doesn't He lift this depression? Why doesn't He intervene to make my marriage a happier one? Just where is God?"

Rather than answering her questions, I raised some of my own. "Jane," I said, "what induced you to come to church on that Sunday morning some months ago? How did you wind up in this particular church that brought about our association? Who was working in my life to bring my training and experience here to this place at this particular time? Why didn't you return to secular counseling that had helped you before instead of coming to the church? Where did you find the confidence to send out your applications, a confidence you had not had before? Who or what enabled you to present yourself in your job interviews in such a way that a prospective employer would agree to hire you? What brought your depression under control so that at least now it doesn't keep you from being completely unproductive? Hasn't the quality of your life improved from what it had been? Did your prayers have anything to do with all this?

Jane went home thinking about these things. When she returned the following week, she had achieved a different perspective. She said, "Thinking about your questions helped me to see that God really has been with me all along. I had been praying and looking for colossal acts that would bring startling changes in my life instantaneously. But God isn't working that way; He is changing things slowly and minutely on a day-to-day basis. Just because He hasn't dealt with all my requests in an instant doesn't mean that He has not dealt with them at all. God is here, and He is at work in my life." Then I was able to talk with Jane about the miracle of the ordinary and she understood my point.

In our losses and the trauma that accompanies them, God works with us through the miracle of the ordinary. We need to have the patience necessary to allow the miracle to unfold and the wisdom to perceive the unfolding. I learned to look for God in my life through the ordinary rather than trying to find the divine hand by waiting upon the extraordinary.

Thinking about the need for patience and wisdom in reacting to God's responses in our life leads to another related understanding that is important to consider. Sometimes we may expect too much from God or we may blame God unjustly, especially when we are being squeezed by life in uncomfortable circumstances, which is a third observation I would make about our living with God through a loss.

We think of God as being all-powerful, and our Creator is omnipotent. That understanding is a part of the doctrine of God that Christian people hold to be true. But in all reality, it is necessary to understand that God is limited in certain ways in what divine love can do for us by the very nature of the system that has been created. God has unilaterally limited that boundless power in order to create a system whose operational mode is to be love.

A real-life example of divine self-limitation that was imposed to serve a higher objective can be seen in the story of Jesus' temptation in the wilderness (Luke 4:1-13). The resurrection was a validation of the ministry of Jesus of Nazareth and the fact that He was, indeed, the Son of God. As such, divine power was operative in and through His life, and the many miracles He performed, including raising people from death, demonstrated this fact. Yet as he fasted in the wilderness for forty days, he refused to use divine powers to satisfy His hunger. Satan tempted Him to do just that saying, "If you are the Son of God, command this stone to become bread." But Jesus replied, "It is written, 'Man shall not live by bread alone.' " The higher purpose to be served in this case was obedience to the mission upon which Jesus was sent. In our case, the higher cause for which God imposes self-limitation on divine power is to make possible our ability to function in the image of God; that is, to be able to give and receive love as God does.

We need to consider how this divine self-limitation impinges upon our relationship with God and how at times we may be unfair in our expectations or our criticism. As discussed in Chapter 6, the ability to love depends upon freedom. By definition, love is something that must be freely given. Love cannot be ordered even by God. If people have no choice in the matter, they cannot be loving beings. In creating men and women to live in a system whose operation-

al mode is designed to be love, the Creator had to grant us
a free will. But as soon as God did that, divine power was
limited in certain ways. Our freedom of choice cannot be
proscribed or our ability to function lovingly will be de-
stroyed.

God's self limitation has implications for what we might
legitimately expect God to do for us even when we are in the
tight places of life like suffering profound loss. Let us examine the reality of that fact.

I would have been very grateful if God could have in some
way relieved me from the pain and agony of losing two sons.
It would be such a relief if divine Love could intervene in the
day-to-day operations of commercial enterprise so as to create jobs for all those who are without work for no reason of
their own making. Think of the hurt that could be avoided
if God could heal the rupture in the lives of people whose
marriages are in trouble. Wouldn't it be wonderful if all our
losses could be averted and all our trauma avoided by the
exercise of God's omnipotence?

But if God begins to intervene directly in each life in such
a way as to do all these things, where does the intervention
stop? Is my miracle to be granted over yours? And if both
are given, in all justice whose prayer can receive a no? Shall
it be the prayer to obliterate poverty, the plea to remove
injustice, or the petition for world peace? And if all such
prayers are to be answered with a divine yes, do we not have
a situation, then, in which life is being divinely manipulated?
How can such prayers be answered without God's arbitrary
intervention in human decisions and behavior? Such direct
and obvious action by the Creator would at once revoke
people's free will. In that event, men and women would be

reduced to mechanical robots; the very thing that operates to define our humanity would be obliterated.

So we cannot have it both ways: an all-powerful God openly intervening in life's processes when that would benefit us individually and, at the same time, a God who does not interfere with the free will that is a mark of our humanity. The two desires are mutually exclusive! As was discussed in Chapter 5, prayer requests should always be made in the context of the understanding "that thy name be glorified" and our expectations always circumscribed by that boundary. In such a stance we can pray for anything that we feel we need from God and our expectations will not be out of bounds.

Now there is a reciprocal aspect to this condition of divine self-limitation: If God cannot always reach down and fix what we pray for, neither has the Creator reached down to arbitrarily "break" us. If we must keep our expectations in bounds, so, too, must we keep in bounds what we blame God for bringing about.

Some folk seem to conceive the Almighty as sitting in heaven before a console pushing buttons to "fix this" or "cause that." When their prayers do not receive a positive response, God is blamed for not being willing to pull the right levers and their trust is withdrawn. In the same fashion, when hardship or grief strike, God is seen as the instigator. Even some faithful Christians will look at a tragedy and declare, "It is God's will." God's will is not to hurt us but to help us grow and develop to what we were created to be. Just as God by self-restriction is restrained from obliterating our free will in order to make all things right for us, neither will God manipulate us to bring punishment or adversity. These things develop out of two facts: One, we are a broken people living in a broken world; and two, there is an evil force at work in the world whose origin and influence we do not completely understand.

I once was called to minister to a family who had just lost a young niece in a tragic accident. After we had talked for awhile and then prayed together, the aunt said to me, "I am so glad that you did not try to tell us that this was God's will. The God I know would never arbitrarily strike down a young life that was so full of potential." I did not tell them that because it wasn't true. The niece was killed through an accidental circumstance, and God had nothing to do with it. But God was crying with this family in their hurt and present to uphold them through their terrible loss. The Creator has established a system which is operating to bring the creation to perfection. God operates within the confines of that system, even to the point of restricting the powers of divine omnipotence, to permit us the gift of an operational free will that really is free.

Now God is not limited in what divine grace wants to do for us and will do for us, but God works in our lives in such a way as to preserve the image in which we were created— beings who are capable of giving and receiving love. In a system whose operational mode is designed to be love, God works to draw us to the divine Self, not through the influence of miracles or the pressure of coercion, but through our free surrender of will in loving response to God's love for us. "I will give them a heart to know that I am the Lord; and they shall be my people and I will be their God, for they shall return to me with their whole heart" (Jer. 24:7).

Keeping in perspective these understandings about God's interaction in our lives can help to generate positive and constructive attitudes rather than negative and destructive ones. Our attitudes are another important aspect of our living with God through our episodes of loss. If we are realistic about how God interacts with us, we can see that God is an ally in such episodes rather than One who ignores our prayers and and metes out punishments to us. If we are unrealistic and, thus, draw the conclusion that God is not with us and working for us, we are led into a state of hopelessness.

Whether we approach our situation in the episodes of profound loss in a positive, hopeful frame of mind or with a negative, defeatist attitude has an important bearing on how we will emerge from the experience. There is an important and growing body of information concerning how our attitudes impinge upon our health, our happiness and our success in life. Claire Safran in an article in *The Reader's Digest,* made the statement, "You are what you think—and if you change your mind—from pessimism to optimism— you can change your life."[2] In that article she discussed a growing body of research, 104 studies involving some 15,000 people, that is proving that positive attitudes can help people be happier and more successful, while negative states of mind lead to hopelessness, sickness, and failure.

As Safran reported, our attitudes impinge on our potential in very practical ways. Her article reported a study done by two researchers at the University of Pennsylvania. Martin Seligman and Peter Schulman investigated the sales representatives of the Metropolitan Life Insurance Company. Their survey found that, among the longtime representatives, those who were positive thinkers sold 37 percent more insurance than did those with negative mental sets. On the basis of those facts, the company hired one hundred people who had failed the standard industry test but scored high as positive thinkers. These individuals, who otherwise would not have been employed, sold 10 percent more insurance than did the average representative working for the company.

The connection between our state of mind and our physical and mental well-being is particularly startling. A new branch of medical science called psychoneuroimmunology focuses on the impact of mental attitudes on the body's resistance to disease. It investigates the links between the mind, the brain, and the immune system. The evidence being gathered supports what doctors have long observed: People who have a fighting spirit have a better chance of recovery than those who give themselves up to their illness.

Donald Robinson reported an incident that occurred at a Connecticut hospital that dramatically demonstrates the connection between attitude and health. Two doctors were making rounds one morning and were at the bedside of a twenty-four-year-old woman who had been in a coma for three months. The chief of neurosurgery commented to the resident physician with him, "Don't waste time on her, she's never going to wake up." Some weeks later the woman did come out of the coma. When asked if she remembered anything, she told the resident, "I remember hearing that doctor say I'd never get well. I made up my mind to show him he was wrong." The physician later commented, "The woman decided to fight for her life and she won. I've seen it happen again and again."[3]

The importance of faith in all this is not lost either. Our attitude toward God can impinge on the degree of hopefulness or despair we exhibit and the amount of fight in our spirit as we face the challenges in our life. Dr. Isaac Djerassi, director of oncology at Mercy Catholic Medical Center in

Philadelphia, was quoted as saying, "We now have convincing evidence that the right mental attitude can help your immune system function more effectively." He went on to point out, "I have treated more than ten thousand people with cancer during the past thirty-three years; the people with faith were always the best fighters."[4]

Thus, keeping in perspective realistic understandings about how God can and does work in our life will tend to support more positive attitudes about God's actual presence with us. It is a way of looking at life through the eyes of faith. The assurance of that presence builds hopefulness because we are convinced that we are not alone. When we have hope, we are inclined to fight against those circumstances that have the potential to drag us down. The evidence indicates that when we fight, our odds against defeat rise substantially. Dr. Norman Vincent Peale has been teaching and preaching about the power in positive thinking for years. Science is now accumulating the evidence that indicates he has been right all along.

As we live with God in our episodes of loss rather than closing ourselves off from that Presence, we find that some positive benefits will come through what is traumatic and upsetting. Now this is not to say that God brings adversity in order that we can derive certain dividends. God does not bring about losses so that we can be convicted of sin and repent or so that we can achieve some other desirable outcomes. The losses we encounter occur because of the system of which we are a part and the brokenness of human society. Since life is designed as a two-stage system having both an earthly and a heavenly phase, since death is the miraculous event in which we are transported from one phase to the other, and since we will suffer the loss of loved ones as a consequence, God will lead us to draw out of the experience things that will be helpful to us and/or to others. Given the fact that our economic system reflects human imperfection and brokenness, and that as a result people will innocently suffer loss of wealth and jobs, God will act to open new insights, new capabilities, or new opportunities through those events. Given the fact that the aging process will eventually bring to each a diminution of our physical and mental powers so that we are not what we used to be and cannot do what we once could do, God will provide compensatory feelings and satisfactions if we are open to perceive them and accept them.

The best examples I can discuss to illustrate the reality that I am talking about here grow out of my own experience with loss which I have shared throughout this book. God did not zap my wife and me by taking away both our sons. Each of those deaths can be understood in the context of the system of which we are a part and the reality of God's interaction with us that has been presented here. But divine grace did operate in my life to bring some positive developments out of my loss that have helped me to survive the experiences and will be of benefit to others with whom I will have contact as my life and ministry continue.

The most obvious and tangible outcome at the moment is this book. The writing of it was a therapy in my own rehabilitation, and I hope it will be of value to others as they meet episodes of loss in their journeys through life. But the book would never have been written in its present form or published had it not been for my second son's death.

I had previously written a manuscript dealing with most of the theological ideas that I have presented here. It was submitted to one publisher after another with corresponding rejection notices following. Finally one editor was gracious enough to explain the problem I was having. "The book is too general," he wrote, "there is no market that we could approach to merchandise it." With that, I ceased my efforts to publish what I had written.

But before my second son died, we shared that tender moment together that I recounted in the opening chapter, that moment in which his love for me was expressed so poignantly in four short words. Those words never left my mind from the moment they were spoken. I said to my wife, "There is some special message that they contain which I do not yet understand for they will not go away." Some weeks later while thinking about my son and those words, the idea began to form that most of what I had previously written had meaning in the context of the loss I was suffering. It was only a step away to realize that those ideas spoke to the issue of all profound loss. It was then that I rewrote the entire work under the inspiration of the words that had given it birth, "Are you upset, Dad?" When it was finished and submitted for publication, it was not long before a publisher indicated an interest in it.

Now that is an example of a very tangible outcome that was a gift of God that came through my episode of loss, but it is not the only example. Because I have experienced what I did, I am a different person and a better minister of the gospel. I know in a deep and profound way the hurt that all of us face in life. Knowing that in a very personal way, I can more realistically empathize with all kinds of loss that people experience and with which, as a pastor, I am called upon to help. I can relate to the hurt of others in a way that is more understanding, more sensitive, and more authentic because the wound I have suffered is one of the most profound.

And with that I have come to the end of what I have to share. As I do, the words of Scripture written by the apostle Paul to the Romans have come to mind,

> Who shall separate us from the love of Christ? Shall tribulation, or distress, or persecution, or famine, or nakedness, or peril, or sword? No, in all these things we are more than conquerors through him who loved us. For I am sure that neither death, nor life, nor angels, nor principalities, nor things present, nor things to come, nor powers, nor height, nor depth, nor anything else in all creation, will be able to separate us from the love of God in Christ Jesus our Lord" (Rom. 8:35,37-79).

With what better words could a story of hope that deals with the reality of God's grace in the episode of loss possibly end?

Notes

CHAPTER 2

1. Lincoln Barnett, *The Universe and Dr. Einstein* (New York: Bantam Books, 1957), p. 14.

2. Gale D. Webbe, *The Night and Nothing* (New York: Harper and Row, 1964), p. 61.

3. M. Scott Peck, *The Road Less Traveled* (New York: Simon and Schuster, 1978), p. 210.

CHAPTER 3

1. Merlin Carothers, *Prison to Praise* (Escondido, Calif.: Merlin R. Carothers, 1970), p. 14.

2. J. G. Pilkington, trans., *Confessions of St. Augustine* (Garden City: International Collectors Library), p. 12.

3. Gale D. Webbe, *The Night and Nothing* (New York: Harper and Row, 1964), p. 73.

4. Henri J. M. Nouwen, *Intimacy* (New York: Harper and Row, 1969), pp. 5-20.

5. Ibid., p. 13.

6. C. S. Lewis, *The Screwtape Letters* (New York: Bantam Books, 1982), p. 22.

CHAPTER 4

1. *Richmond Times Herald* 4 Nov. 1979)

2. Merlin Carothers, *Prison to Praise* (Escondido, Calif.: Merlin R. Carothers, 1970), p. 64.

3. Armando Valladares, *Against All Hope: The Prison Memoirs of Armando Valladares* (New York: Alfred A. Knofp, Inc., 1986).

4. Wayne G. Rollins, *Jung and the Bible* (Atlanta: John Knox Press, 1983).

5. M. Scott Peck, *The Road Less Traveled* (New York: Simon and Schuster, 1978), p. 269.

6. Ibid., p. 260.

7. Kyle Duncan, and Mike Yorkey, "They, Too, Traveled the Road to Damascus." Reprinted from "Focus On the Family," magazine (Apr. 1987). Copyright ©, 1987, Focus on the Family, Pomona, CA 91799. All rights reserved. International copyright secured. Used by permission.

CHAPTER 5

1. Ole Hallesby, *Prayer* (Minneapolis: Augsburg Publishing House, 1959).

CHAPTER 7

1. Gerhard Adler, ed., *The Collected Works of C. G. Jung* (Princeton: Princeton University Press, 1953-1978), 3:292.

2. Eric Bern, *A Layman's Guide to Psychiatry and Psychoanalysis* (New York: Simon and Schuster, 1968), p. 88.

3. M. Scott Peck, *The Road Less Traveled* (New York: Simon and Schuster, 1978), pp. 239-240.

4. Peck, M. Scott, *People of the Lie* (New York: Simon and Schuster, 1983), p. 39.

5. Peck, *The Road,* p. 283.

6. Nouwen, Henri J.M., *Intimacy* (New York: Harper and Row, 1969), p. 29.

CHAPTER 8

1. Jack Murphy, "Filling the Void." Reprinted from The Full Gospel Business Men's *Voice,* August 1987.

2. Ibid.

3. Ibid.

4. Ibid.

5. A. M. Forsyth, and A. M. de Commaille, eds., *Prayers Michel Quoist* (New York: Avon Books, 1963), pp. 139-140. Used with permission of Sheed & Ward, 115 E. Armour Blvd., Kansas City, MO.

6. Robert C. Leslie, *Man's Search for a Meaningful Faith* (Nashville: Graded Press, 1967), Selection #144

7. Albert Schweitzer, *The Quest for the Historical Jesus* (New York: The MacMillan Co., 1959), p. 403.

CHAPTER 9

1. Robert C. Leslie, *Man's Search for a Meaningful Faith* (Nashville: Graded Press, 1967), Selection #87.

2. Excerpted with permission from "You Are What You Think" by Claire Safran, *The Reader's Digest,* August 1987. Copyright © 1987 by The Reader's Digest Assn., Inc.

3. Excerpted with permission from "Your Attitude Can Make You Well" by Donald Robinson, *The Reader's Digest,* April 1987. Copyright © 1987 by The Reader's Digest Assn., Inc.

4. Ibid.